T0147007

The Significance of Existence

Second Edition 2019

TOM & TAMRA BENNETT

BALBOA.
PRESS

A DIVISION OF HAY HOUSE

Balboa Press books may be ordered through booksellers or by contacting:

Balboa Press
A Division of Hay House
1663 Liberty Drive
Bloomington, IN 47403
www.balboapress.com
1 (877) 407-4847

Print information available on the last page.

ISBN: 978-1-9822-1344-2 (sc)
ISBN: 978-1-9822-1345-9 (e)

Balboa Press rev. date: 12/28/2018

MISSION STATEMENT

Give the truth to the world. Let it be received where it will. Many will read the messages. Some will accept the truth, others will read through curiosity, a few will ridicule. Yet to all is the truth given and to all remains the power of choice.

The hope of the world in these times is in spiritualizing all forms of activity—promoting understanding through love and service. These must be the watchwords if the world is to come into lasting peace. We are trying to influence a world that is going astray and could cause undreamed of suffering. We are trying to overcome the thought of materialists and to bring a spiritual outlook into the earthly life. We need the help of all on earth who can think in spiritual terms. The great battle to be fought now is between the spiritual and the material, between idealism and carnalism. You can help by spreading the word. We are asking that you help because the battle may be long and the victory far away.

Halls of Light is not allied with any sect, denomination, political entity, or organization. We neither endorse nor oppose any cause. There are no dues for membership. Halls of Light is self-supporting through its own voluntary contributions. Halls of Light has but one purpose: to help through encouragement and understanding...

DEDICATION

For H. F. Kurdi, a forward thinker in a dangerous place and time
and
Richard F. Hagen who, upon his passing, was asked the bewildering question: "Why do we die?"

'Look deeper into Nature and then you will understand everything better.' - Albert Einstein

INTRODUCTION

This work serves as another superb example and unique perspective, bringing facts and ideas together to manifest the unity of the cosmos and the universal human experience.

Life is immortal. It never had a beginning and never had an end, but it possesses the power of development.

All sentient beings are Immortal Spiritual Beings. This includes human beings. For the sake of accuracy and simplicity, we use a made-up word: "IS-BE" because the primary nature of an immortal being is that we live in a timeless state of "is", and the only reason for our existence is that we decide to "be".

When you look at a Man, you see nothing before you but a Man composed of skin, or epidermis. If you trusted to nothing but your eyes without reason, you could not say that Man was composed of anything but skin.

Now there is the perfect form of a Man composed of skin. Underneath the epidermis is the true skin, which is to the sight invisible. So there is another perfect form of Man, composed of true skin. Underneath the true skin is another perfect form composed of veins. Take away all else and there stands the Man of veins.

Next, there is the perfect arterial Man. Next, there stands the perfect form of Man composed of nerves. Now we have the perfect form of Man composed of muscles. Then there stands the perfect form of Man composed of bones, a skeleton.

All this is matter, or material substance which would be inert, or dead if it were not for an animating principle that permeated every particle of this complex structure. *That animating principle is the perfect Spiritual Man.*

This spiritual form is composed of magnetism and electricity. These two are the immortal, imperishable forms of Man. They are united and go hand-in-hand. *One cannot exist without the other.*

There is a third principle which is called **The Soul of Man. The magnetic form and the electric form bear the soul within them.** The soul is the guiding principle of the spiritual body. It clothes itself with magnetism and electricity. That is, it holds it together in the perfect form of Man. **When the soul leaves the material body of Man, it takes the magnetic and electric body with it, for these three bodies are inseparable.**

If Man did not have a magnetic and an electric body, there would be no heat within him for *it is the uniting of magnetism and electricity that causes all light and heat.*

When the soul leaves the material body of a Man and has taken with it all the magnetism and electricity, the material body falls apart or decays, for its animating principle has left it—-*all that could think, hear, feel or see has left it.*

Now this that has left the material body we call the spiritual body. *It is triune in its nature—-the intelligent body, the magnetic body and the electric body.*

This body has lost nothing but a gross covering of matter which it no longer needs. All that thinks, hears, sees or feels, it retains, for these are of the soul and not of the material body. If they were, the material body would still continue to think, hear, feel and see just the same as when the soul had fled.

The soul has an electric and a magnetic body. The magnetic and the electric body are perfectly and evenly balanced—*they are in exact equilibrium. They are the clothing and the vehicles of the soul.*

These three bodies in one are all invisible to the material sight of Man because they are composed of invisible substance, for all know that electricity is invisible and magnetism is invisible and the soul is invisible. Under certain conditions, this body may be visible.

The soul is the intelligent, or animating principle of the magnetic and electric body. It can move its electric body with the swiftness of electricity or it can gently float or remain quiescent. *The magnetic body attracts and holds together the electric body, for the magnetic body permeates the electric body and the intelligent soul permeates and guides the whole.*

If Man is immortal, so are all things else. Life is spirit and spirit is immortal in whatever form it may exist. The tiniest blade of grass is just as immortal as Man. No form, when once attained, is ever resolved back into elementary principles. Matter falls away from it, but the form is retained forever. If Man develops and ripens for immortality through the materiality, so do all things else that have life whatever their kind. All things die, or cast off their material covering. It is against all reason to suppose that Man is alone in his immortality. In order to explain Man's immortality, we must explain how worlds are made, what the Spirit of All Things is and how everything in its material form must yield up its spirit and why.

We begin with the space that holds life or the Spirit of all Things, the space that carries life onward forever and ever. We start with ether…

CONTENTS

ETHER

The medium permeating all space

Ether (ēthēr) is a great and profound abstraction, the medium permeating all space and transmitting transverse light like waves. Consider it as air of fine, fine substance.

There is no such thing as "nothing". There never was any such thing as nothing. All things originate within the atmosphere or ether. There is not anything which **originates** within earthly matter.

For instance, if nothing intervened between earth and the nearest planet, there would be no distance between the earth and that planet. **There are millions of miles of something between or there could not be millions of miles of distance.** This something is the substance called ether or the ethereal atmosphere. The earth's atmosphere does not entirely constitute these miles, for that does not extend even one thousand miles. Distance is simply that which lies between. Atmosphere may not be and is not the proper word but ether, or ethereal substance is.

As ethereal substance can be measured and calculated by miles, and as all space is filled by this ethereal substance, these vast distances have **something** within them. They hold the sublimated essences of all things that grow or live on the earth, *including the elementary principles that produce all material things*. The ethereal atmosphere permeates the earth's atmosphere, including the spaces between the atoms.

What was thought to be "void" is really ether. This ether fills all space, penetrating in and through all things. The ether is filled by spiritual, celestial and material bodies or forms. These forms differ in both shape and density. *All space is filled by four great first principles: ether* (spiritual substance), *matter* (solid substance), *magnetic flame and germinal points.* This ether holds the life, or spirit of all things and carries it onward for ever and ever. Ether is something that can never change it's form or consistency, and the great ethereal ocean is endless.

All things that *are*, float and move and exist within the ethereal sea that gives birth to worlds and systems of worlds. *This is the ocean of eternity. Out of it, all things are formed that ever were or ever shall be. It ever has been. It ever will be…*

ATOMS

The coalescing of two points

Within the ethereal sea is the atomic sea consisting of small round globes or atoms which are swimming or moving within it.

The atomic sea completely fills the ethereal sea, yet the ethereal sea completely surrounds each atom so that no one atom absolutely touches another atom. **The atoms are a shade heavier and more dense than the ether,** yet the atom is counterpoised and evenly balanced by a third principle at its very heart or central point which is a pure flame, pale amber in color. Just a point or dot of pure magnetic flame and, like the yoke within an egg, is surrounded by elastic, translucent matter. The composition of this matter is just one half water. Each atom may be divided into three equal component parts: one third magnetic flame (which is the pure spirit of the atom) one third pure water and the other third solid substance (which is eventually to be chemicalized into *everything that exists on earth*).

The little invisible flame is called **magnetism:** the eternal motive power, the great pulsing heart of all things. Magnetism is a pure, invisible, spiritual flame. The little flame is the central point or nucleus of the atom. The coalescing of the two principles **matter and magnetism** generates heat or a little magnetic flame within the atom which heats the atom to a white heat. **Therefore, heat is the coalescing of magnetism and matter.**

The spirit of the atom is the little magnetic flame within each atom. **The vast ocean of spirit and matter are counterparts.** Each little flame of magnetism attracts and holds an equal proportion of matter which makes the perfect atom.

Magnetic flame exists in minute points. Each point of magnetic flame is always attracting and holding to itself a point of matter within which it hides and covers itself. The coalescing of these two points forms a perfect atom.

In earth life, these atoms are invisible. They are so ethereal in their nature that they belong to the octave above human sight. Atoms as well as worlds are never at rest, for nothing remains status quo, but they are in constant motion. Each tiny atom is revolving in its own particular orbit. **The little flame or spirit within the heart of the atom is a magnet, or magnetic attraction.**

GERMS

Points consisting of all things which live and grow.

The ethereal sea is also filled with germinal points constituting a germinal sea.

All things start from an invisible point. This law holds good without a single exception. *Space is an ocean of matter, spirit, germinal points and ether.* The great ethereal ocean is endless and filled with germinal points, magnetic points of flame and translucent matter.

All germs exist in minute points and roll together in great waves within the never-ending ethereal sea. All things whatever start from a germinal point. These germinal points consist of and contain all things which live and grow. The spiritual germs of everything in existence, or that ever did or ever will exist, are forever within the ethereal atmosphere. *All life originates within the atmosphere or ether.* All life, whatever it's kind, exists in germinal points or life germs, or soul germs, all meaning the same thing.

All things grow. All things come forth from a germ. This is the first great natural law that has no exceptions. *The second great law is male and female, positive and negative.* Every germ is positive and negative or male *and* female. Here again, there is not one exception throughout all nature's domain. Nothing in nature springs forth from one parent alone. *There never was a Man born on earth who did not have a father and a mother.* There never existed an animal that did not have a father and a mother, not an insect, not a worm, not a fish in the sea.

Some of the very lowest life bears the male and female in one form, but the principle is precisely the same. The same principle holds good in all vegetable life. The atoms that compose rocks and the soil hold the male and female principle within each one.

There is not one exception to this great law. Whenever Man finds a law that has no exceptions, he may commence at one end of the chain and follow it as far as his reason can go and he will make no mistakes.

And here is another great, unchangeable law: *every world is round or egg-shaped—-a circle: every world moves in an orbit, egg-shaped or elliptical. An atom is elliptical in form. All germs are egg-shaped and all germs are developed into eggs, whether within bird, fish, beast or Man. Man's head is egg-shaped; Man's brain is egg-shaped.*

You may see spiritual germs with the naked eye. Sit quietly in a room and look toward the light of a window. Look out the window towards the sky, but let your gaze rest steadily upon the atmosphere a few yards from the eyes.

Do not look at anything but the air. Gaze quietly and steadily for a few moments and you will behold the germinal sea, consisting of living, germinal points of light. These points of light vary in size from those about as large as the point of a pin to those of a much larger size, the size of the head of a pin.

The points of light which you see are living little globes, lighter in color than the atmosphere, of all grades and sizes. They are darting here and there in all directions, filled with life in motion, never still for an instant. Little, bright, translucent globes of light. An unending sea of germinal life...

MAGNETISM

The cause of an effect.

Magnetism is a real substance, consisting of minute points of pure, invisible ethereal or spiritual flame. We live in a world of cause and effect. Like the wind, magnetism is not visible to the material eye but the *effect* is visible. It is the light and heat of magnetism and electricity that man sees and feels. There can be no effect without an adequate cause. Magnetism is the cause of an effect. The universe is dual in nature, positive (male) and negative (female).

There are *two forces in* magnetism: the positive or "pull" force and an equal and opposite "push" or negative force.

Mathematically: $1 (+) + 1 (-) = 0$

Zero represents "balance" and not "nothing" because in the world of "things" there cannot be no "no-thing".

Magnetism is the spirit within all...

HOW WORLDS ARE MADE

Nothing is produced from only one parent.

If we find out how one earth came into existence, we shall find out how all earths, planets and the heavens came into being. If we find out how one apple grows, we shall discover how all apples grow.

It is a self-evident truth that the apple was never made out of nothing but it has within itself just as much substance as composes it. An earth has as much substance as composes *it* and is **not** made out of nothing.

Crush or squeeze an apple and see that it is made out of fluid and solid. The apple obtains the substance composing it from the tree on which it grows. The tree springs forth from a small seed which is placed a little way beneath the soil and the little seed holds within it *a living spiritual germ,* an exact miniature copy, invisible and spiritual, of the tree that is to be developed from it.

The tree strikes its roots deep into the earth and raises its arms aloft into the heavens. The tree is the parent of the apple and the apple, or seed of the apple, is the parent of the tree. *So does the earth grow.*

All earths grow from a parent tree, yet the parent of the earth is not in the form of a tree but in the form of a globe.

The earth is not the tree and the tree is not the apple but the earth must first exist that the tree may exist, and the tree exists to bring forth the apple. *That is a self-evident truth that cannot be contradicted.*

As the apple is not the tree, but the *product* of the tree, *so the earth from which we come is the product of a parent globe.*

It is a self-evident fact that the tree produces the apple. If you give an apple to a child that has never seen a tree that produced apples and say "This apple grew on a tree", the boy in his ignorance, might say "That is only a supposition, I don't believe it! God made this apple out of nothing." When you take the child and lead him to a tree on which apples grow, then he is convinced of the truth of what you say.

Nothing is produced from only one parent. The apple is not produced from one parent alone; neither are the earth and planets produced from one parent alone.

The earth has for its parents the sun, the sun's magnetic counterpart and the great eternal ocean of matter and spirit as it exists now, as it has ever existed and as it ever will exist.

Within the spirit dwells another principle which we shall call God or force, or power, or will. It makes little difference what we call it. *It is the power that moves all the rest. And this is God!* It is the only God that is made manifest.

The sun, as the trees, the apple and the earth, grew from a little seed buried within the vast ocean of matter. Each apple produces its own seed, and there the circle is complete. The seed produces the tree, the tree the apple and the apple the seed.

The seed of the apple is produced from a living spiritual germ that the petals of the flower grasp from out of the atmosphere or from out of the heavens or in other words, from out of the vast ocean of spirit and matter.

As with one blossom, it is with all. Within the petals of the blossom is a little magnetic cup that attracts and holds in its embrace an invisible germ which exists within the ethereal atmosphere, or spiritual atmosphere. The petals of the flower close over it, the magnetic attraction holds it. It is the seed, the *spirit of the seed* and without it no seed can come forth.

So the apple does not in reality produce the seed, *but the petals of the flower of the tree; yet, the petals are worthless without the spiritual germ.*

As applies to the sun, first the seed of a sun exists forever within the vast ocean of spirit and matter. *It is a little invisible magnetic, or spiritual flame, or germ* which attracts matter and holds it fast until it becomes a perfect atom. Then it attracts other atoms *like itself* until a small globe is formed about the size of a goose egg. *This is the real material seed of a sun, the visible nucleus.* And there are countless nuclei, or perfect seeds of suns that are all destined to take root and grow into perfect suns in the vast ocean of matter and spirit.

The seed of an apple grows into a large and perfect tree by the power of attracting and appropriating atom after atom to its own use and benefit.

So the nucleus of the sun grows by its power of attracting and gathering to itself atom after atom as it rolls through the vast ocean of matter and spirit.

An apple is composed of solid and fluid and it is a soft, smooth globe. So the body of a sun that is to be is composed of solid and fluid and it is a soft, smooth globe.

Like the apple, it is equally and evenly mixed together. But this young sun, unlike the apple, is revolving with great rapidity in space, gathering and growing, gathering and growing until the time arrives when it has reached an enormous size.

The first, or primary forms that exist within the vast ocean of spirit and matter are very much like a goose egg without a shell. These 'eggs' are all in rapid motion, thrown here and there on the waves of the atomic sea. This conglomeration of atoms quivers and trembles like a ball of jelly or, in substance, like a round jellyfish, transparent and slightly tinged with yellow.

This ball commenced with one atom within the atomic sea. It has attracted and held atoms enough to form a ball, which is the first form or nucleus of a sun. The little magnetic flame, or point of fire within each atom, attracts and holds together this ball of translucent matter. The ball will keep on rolling and attracting atoms and holding them until a globe is formed as large as the sun.

From a small nucleus, this immense globe has grown by its constant motions and revolutions, by attracting and holding atom after atom. The globe is soft and warm, although it has grown to an enormous size. It has become a little harder than a ball of jelly. It is now about the consistency of an apple and very much the same color as an apple without its skin. Its own motion, weight and growth has hardened it. It is warm, for each little atom still holds its central magnetic flame. Thus the cold, translucent matter is warmed throughout all this great mass. It bears its life, growth and heat within it, just as a little animal does when it is growing rapidly. This young, or primary world grows very rapidly, much more rapidly than one would suppose.

It feeds and grows from outside sustenance, just as a plant or animal does: it constantly gathers atoms and appropriates them to its own use and benefit, the only difference being that, like a snowball, it gathers as it rolls.

It rolls within the atomic sea and holds to itself every atom with which it comes in contact. *But it only gathers the atoms which are composed of magnetic flame and translucent matter*: the ethereal and germinal seas are left intact. And, it has robbed and appropriated all the atoms within the space wherein it has moved. In this way, it creates a vast orbit for itself, for it still continues to roll where it can gather its food. It shuns that part of the sea which it has deprived of its atoms, for *it attracts the atoms and the intact atomic sea attracts it. This is the manner in which the first or primary worlds create their own orbit.*

At length, this immense globe, rolling within its vast orbit, ceases to grow. It has reached a point in its career where it must drop a portion of its weight: *it has become too weighty to hold itself together any longer. The law of attraction and growth* ceases with it. Its weight and rapid motion causes the outer surface to harden but the inner part remains soft. It now presents more the appearance of an orange with its rind, the harder and softer part being about in the same proportion, and, as it still rapidly revolves within its orbit, the inner part gradually becomes loosened from the rind. As the inner part becomes loose, the motions of the now two distinct bodies are not the same. The inner part, being softer and warmer than the rind by its more rapid motion, constantly drives off or repels the rind, thus causing the rind to crack open. This primary world has but two motions, the revolving on its own axis and the rolling in its rut or orbit. It has become elliptical, or in the form of an egg, and thus the shell cracks all around its central part.

The intact globe within still rolls on and, for a certain period of time, the shell or ring is still carried along with it by the power of attraction. But there comes a time when the ring, by its own weight and the constantly repelling motion of the central globe, breaks all in pieces and falls away from the inner globe. The inner globe escapes entirely and still rolls on by itself.

These globes, by their motion, repel each other and keep each other at just the proper distance. And yet, their power of attraction holds each other at just the proper distance. The ring which has been cast off from the parent globe becomes of harder and firmer consistency than the first globe and, as it draws itself together at its central point, its surface lies in great fissures and chasms: that is, its surface is all cracked into pieces.

The parent globe's position and orbit lies about midway of the space that has been robbed of its atoms. That is, *it occupies a central position and the first planet or ring moves in a great circle around it.*

But the first planet's orbit is constantly growing larger and larger as it again goes on attracting atoms and again adds to its own weight. The planet will keep on revolving and throwing as many globes as it is capable of.

This eventually becomes a system of worlds, the sun being the first or primary world. *All suns are first, or primary worlds.* All earths or planets are secondary worlds, all differing somewhat from each other. *These are the children of the sun.*

The sun is composed of atoms. *At the center of each atom is a little magnetic flame, a point of pure magnetism.* After a sun throws off all its children, it begins to grow old and, at length, dies or yields up its spirit. And, as each atom is composed equally of spirit and matter, therefore *spirit and matter are the parents of a sun.* The uniting, or marriage of the two, produces other worlds. But the sun must, at length, yield up its spirit.

As there are fundamental notes in music, so each system of worlds has fundamental planets. All the others are auxiliary, or aids to the first or primary worlds. *All space and time is filled with these worlds in their various stages of perfection and growth.*

Looking at a complete system of planets, the first, or primary globe and the smaller rings or globes which it has cast off, the parent globe is of immense size compared with the rings which it has thrown off, yet it is comparatively soft and warm at first. This primary globe has now passed the stage of reproduction. She has become too hard and dense throughout all her vast body. She moves more slowly than at first. Her orbit has become extremely large. She has ceased to attract and hold atoms, for the atoms of which she is composed have become more hardened and amalgamated. She has settled down into a more metallic form. And now, instead of attracting atoms, she repulses them, or they glide off her surface more as water glides off glass. She has not become hard as glass, but her relation to the soft, translucent, primary atom is comparatively that of glass and water.

A revolving planet of glass cannot hold water on its surface. She has passed the period of her youth and growth. She has passed the period of reproduction and is now preparing for a new, more useful and glorious life.

This globe has never had an atmosphere. She has never evolved water. She has never had any light of her own except the pale light of amber which her inner or magnetic flame has given to her. She is composed equally of amber flame and matter.

She has now become old and is about to die, or yield up her spirit. Her spirit is the magnetic flame that lies at the heart of every atom that composes her vast body. Her children are yet in darkness: they have no material light, only a pale magnetic light like that of their mother. Yet their light is not as powerful as is that of her, for they are broken and uneven over all their surface, while she is as smooth as glass.

To Man, these worlds in their primary condition would appear to be in darkness without any atmosphere, without any water and about as hard as kneaded dough. Their entire bodies are of the same consistency and very much like dough.

These planets are now all revolving in their own orbits within the vast space which has been robbed of its atoms, the first planet rolling on the outermost limits of this space. But this space has only been robbed of its atoms. These planets are rolling within an ethereal and germinal sea, for the ethereal and germinal sea remains intact. It is as yet only flame and matter that have coalesced and produced form in the shape of vast globes. Each little atom is in the form of a globe. All creation is in the form of globes or circles. As the first planet continually moves outward in a spiral orbit, so all things run in spiral circles.

Up to this point, the sun had no light of its own. It did not shine. *Before the sun could shine it must have yielded up every particle of its spirit or magnetic flame to become a mass of black carbon.*

For ages the sun was dying, or yielding up its spirit. But as all spirit retains the exact form of the body which it has left, *the sun's spirit retained the exact shape of the sun and became its invisible magnetic counterpart.*

The material body of the sun still retained its form, so the dark body of the sun and its magnetic counterpart form a perfect electric battery.

Magnetism is forever setting the dark body of the sun in a blaze of light. Thus, light and heat exist!

The light of the sun is easily understood when we find out the cause of light of any kind. The same law that causes light of any kind causes the light of our sun and of all other suns.

Two great principles must be combined to cause light of any kind. Those principles are the conjunction of magnetism and carbon. *Magnetism is pure, ethereal or spiritual flame,* and carbon is an opposing elementary substance. When magnetism touches carbon, electricity is the result. *Electricity is light and heat.* Therefore the light of the sun is electrical. In other words, *the sun is an electric light!*

The body of the sun is a mass of black carbon, a globe that has died, or yielded up its spiritual flame, which was pure magnetism. Pure magnetism is invisible to Man. The spirit, which the sun has yielded up, is its invisible counterpart, in form precisely like the sun.

The black body of carbon rolls in a vast orbit. Its magnetic counterpart rolls in the same orbit, keeping perfect step with the carbonic globe, but *always lying exactly opposite each other.*

The spiritual magnetic globe is continually sending great waves of pure magnetism to the sun or black body of carbon which causes electricity to leap forth at every point.

There rolls the great electric light: the sun. *Every spark of electricity leaps back to the magnetic globe and is again resolved into pure magnetism.* And thus the great battery forever plays back and forth.

The sun was the child of two great principles: magnetism and matter, or spirit and matter or male and female. All existing forms in nature are caused by the *uniting* **of spirit and matter.**

Form is the result, or child, of spirit and matter: but children must grow, as all things must grow. Nothing leaps forth at once full grown but always begins as a little germinal point, or atom. So the great eternal ocean that exists throughout all time and space is pure magnetism and translucent matter. These atoms lie within the ethereal sea and *ether is coexistent with spirit and matter.*

Thus primary worlds start from an invisible point. Points of magnetic flame attract and hold around themselves an equal amount of matter, and this forms atoms.

Suns, which are primary worlds, start from one atom. One atom, through the attractive power of the magnetic flame within it, attracts other atoms and holds them by the power of attraction and cohesion until an enormous globe rolls within the ethereal sea. This globe is soft and when it has become extremely large, it must, from necessity, cast off rings that form the planets which are the children of the sun.

The germinal points within the ethereal sea are yet left intact; *it is only magnetic flame and matter that enter into the composition of the first or primary worlds.*

When the sun has thrown off as many rings as it is capable of doing, it at length, grows old and yields up its magnetic flame or spirit. *The result is light and heat.*

Nothing is forever fixed; the eternal is growth, and not fixture; motion, and not inactivity. Every world in space is in rapid motion. Everything upon the earth is in motion. All vegetation is growing or decaying. Even the rocks that seem so substantial are constantly moldering, changing and, at length, turning to soil. The soil is constantly springing up to clothe animal and vegetable life.

The law of motion and growth has no exceptions.

The suns are not inhabited worlds. A tree is not an apple, but the parent of an apple. It exists first that the apple may exist. *So, a sun is not for purposes of habitation but for the purpose of giving birth to worlds that are to be inhabited* after it has become a spiritualized world to fit those other worlds, its children, for habitation.

The inhabited planets (earths) were thrown off from the suns. *The suns,* after they had yielded up their spirits, *became magnetic batteries of electric light and heat.*

The earth was made as the shell (which was thrown off from the sun, being somewhat harder than the real body of the sun), in gathering itself together by the law of attraction at its central point, in order that it might become a round globe, cracked in pieces on its surface. It became seamed and ridged everywhere. It was yet equally mixed together, solid and fluid and, of course was still very soft. At this time it had neither water nor atmosphere. As an apple appears to be rather a hard body until it is squeezed, so the earth was squeezed or baked that its water might appear.

As soon as the sun became a blazing body of light and heat, its rays struck this immature earth. As the earth had no atmosphere to shield it, it began to bake and harden very rapidly. As it thus hardened, the water was entirely squeezed out from the solid parts and the solid part at length became solid rock.

Water and all other things seek their own level. The water ran down and filled up all the chasms and fissures of the earth. Now the earth, instead of being soft like an apple and equally mixed, was nothing but solid rock and water. But there was no atmosphere.

The earth being then young, was much nearer the sun than it is at the present time, for all planets as they become mature and more perfect, recede from their parents as all apples when they are ripe leave the tree and as all children leave their parents.

The earth, lying very near the sun, was intensely hot. The rocks were like coals of fire. And the waters all became seething cauldrons.

A dense vapor surrounded the earth about three miles in thickness. This was an antidote for the intense heat. Within this water, or vapor, the air resided and was evolved from it.

As the earth gradually receded from the sun and the vapor condensed and cooled, great storms arose. Terrible deluges and rushing whirlwinds; forked lightnings constantly split the rocks asunder and many of the pieces were hurled with awful force into the chasms. This was only perfecting the earth and rendering it more evenly balanced.

At length, all things took on a milder form. The water was now comparatively cool. The action of the rains and the waters kept wearing away at the rocks and as they pulverized and separated the substances that composed the rocks, the waters carried these substances along in their embrace.

As like attracts like, the metallic substances settled in mines or beds by themselves. But salt and lime and many other substances were soluble in water and the water retained these.

At length, the waters levelled the rocks to the extent that an ocean was formed. After awhile, the waters of the earth, which was receding farther and farther away from the sun, became cool enough for life to make its appearance upon the earth. The rocks were so cool that moss and small ferns began to form upon them. Sponge, jellyfish and snails began to form within the sea. Then maggots, worms, insects and reptiles gradually were evolved, one from the other. Then butterflies and small birds.

The ocean is gradually and constantly changing its bed. As the ocean receded, it left rich alluvial soil which brought forth rank tropical vegetation. At length, vast forests were filled with wild animals. Then the ape, and from it the low, squat savage appeared. From this, Man gradually arose to his present estate.

Now after the water had yielded up its atmosphere, the atmosphere in its turn yielded up its ethereal, or spiritual atmosphere. *This is the first spiritual atmosphere that surrounds the earth.*

The earths and the first spiritual spheres around them are the lowest. From them are being gradually evolved the higher heavens.

The spaces between the worlds, *beyond the spheres of earth,* contain great magnetic waves of a spiritual sea. It is a vast ocean of pure amber flame, rolling in waves all in one direction, toward the sun. It is a pure magnetic sea, devoid of matter and its destination is the sun.

The sun, like ourselves, is actually but one sun in two forms, male and female; magnetism and electricity.

Traveling as fast as electricity and light can travel, we find on the sun's magnetic counterpart, a great chemical laboratory. Every ray of light and heat which the sun shoots forth travels directly to this magnetic globe and is there again resolved into magnetism proper, to roll back again in great waves to the sun.

This magnetic globe is invisible to Man, as all magnetism is. The electric body of the sun is also invisible to Man. *It is the result or effect that is visible.*

It is the light and heat of magnetism and electricity that Man sees and feels, for the light and heat of the sun strikes and bathes in glory all the planets that lie between it and its counterpart. The great magnetic waves, as they roll towards the sun, strike and bathe and nourish all the planets that lie between it and the sun.

The moon, belonging to the earth, is a child of the earth. Not a spiritual child, but a material child. All things toil together to bring forth intelligent, imperishabl*e angels*. The sun is a type of the "angelic" world. The true male and female are blended into oneness *yet they are two distinct bodies* making one perfect or complete "angel". Angels are constantly emitting rays of wisdom, love and truth and forever performing all manner of good works. Therefore, the earth brought forth Man who is eventually to become an intelligent angel. All things on earth, and the earth itself, must yield up their spirit and go on to make the spiritual and heavenly realms in which the spirit and angels may dwell.

When an atom within the composition of earth has once yielded up *its* spirit, it can't be replenished on earth. It is worthless and drifts about at the mercy of a higher law. It has lost its power of attraction and of being attracted. The atmosphere takes it up, carries it and thrusts it out beyond its limit.

There are countless millions of these atoms rising continually. When they get beyond the atmosphere, they crowd and push each other until they lie in a helpless mass, or belt or in two or three belts as the planet Jupiter.

There is a law by which these atoms are replenished or revivified and spiritual essence put back into them. These worthless atoms must be replenished in some way. All the other atoms in space are filled with spirit. They cannot be robbed. Each atom has only enough for itself and will repulse the worthless ones.

Comets are not the nucleus' of other worlds, but torches: great magnetic torches, vast oceans of pure spiritual essence devoid of matter. They circle and sweep around among the planets and *revivify every worthless atom* with which they come into contact.

These atoms have again received the spiritual essence. They have the power of attracting and of being attracted. They weld themselves together in the form of a ring, such as around the planet Saturn.

After this has taken place a great many times, the ring becomes very large and heavy and the earth, or planet, by its motion, is constantly repulsing and throwing it off. At length it breaks in pieces.

Then by its own inherent power of attraction, it draws itself together at its central point; and its surface is all in great yawning chasms, fissures and mountains. But it is soft as the apple; yet it has become an independent orb and commences its own revolutions. The earth holds it at the proper distance and there rolls the moon which stays in its orbit.

Our earth is young, it has but one moon. Jupiter is older, it has many moons. Thus the planets go on. By this time they have yielded up their entire spirit and have developed moons and spiritual spheres

When the earths have accomplished this, the remnants of matter which are left, broken and robbed in part of their spirit, fall in pieces. These are the asteroids. These pieces in turn fall in pieces and drop as meteors into some other planet. The asteroids are gradually dropping in pieces in this way and sending meteors and meteoric showers onto the earths.

The finite earth is a type of the infinite: it is composed of fire, earth and water. Out of the ethereal sea springs forth all things that are, or have been or ever shall be: suns, moons and stars; constellations and systems and zones of worlds; angels and archangels.

Within this sea, which extends throughout all space and time, lie the germs of all possible things yet in the undeveloped germinal state. This is the material out of which all existent things are formed. It is the uniting, or marriage of the magnetic flame and the translucent matter that gives birth to all form.

A WORLD IN THE ACT OF YIELDING UP ITS SPIRIT

All nature is evolved or separated, one thing from another.

Recall how the large globe, after casting off rings, grew old and must at length yield up its spirit. Here is a system whereby the primary globe, or sun, is yielding up its spirit, which is it's magnetic flame:

Pale magnetic rays shoot out from every atom composing the body of the vast globe. The reason is that the globe is becoming too dense to hold its flame. That is, the flame cannot be compressed and, as the globe condenses by its own motion and weight, the flame is squeezed out of it, something as one would take an orange or an apple in one's hand and gradually squeeze it until all the juice was squeezed out. Only in the case of the globe, it is magnetic flame instead of juice. *It takes ages to yield up it's spirit.*

These magnetic rays, or the spirit of the atoms composing the globe, cannot enter into any other atoms, for they are full and perfect in themselves. Consequently, as like attracts like by natural law, they gather themselves together (for there is nothing else they can do) into a form by themselves just like the globe which they have left or been squeezed out of.

Every particle of magnetic flame has left the body of the globe and has gathered itself into a corresponding **magnetic globe**. The two globes now lie opposed to each other or at opposite points, the magnetic globe rolling in the same orbit as the globe which has yielded it up.

The dead globe is now black as night and is a mass of carbon. When the magnetic globe has become perfected and gathered up its last ray, and the globe of carbon has become condensed to a proper consistency, **the carbon globe holds a powerful attraction for the magnetic globe.** And now a glorious thing is about to take place: The carbonic globe attracts great waves of magnetism from the magnetic globe. **It sets the carbon on fire and there rolls a great and glorious sun!** Every ray of light and heat which the sun throws off passes straight back to the magnetic globe and they forever keep up the play for countless ages.

When the light and heat from the sun strike the magnetic globe, they are again changed into pure magnetic flame and again thrown back in great waves which bathe and set on fire the carbon at every point.

The two globes forever roll on exactly opposite each other, both in the same orbit. **And there is the great electric light: a sun.** The magnetic globe is not visible to the material eyes of Man, only the electric light, the light of the sun which is in reality a dead world that has yielded up its spirit. The spirit has become its counterpart and is an outgrowth of itself which constantly sets it in a blaze of glory.

The sun has no atmosphere. It is a first, or primary world never intended for habitation. It gives light and heat to the secondary worlds to which it has given birth. These secondary worlds are still very soft at this point, about as soft as kneaded dough. They were rings cast off from the body of the sun. In gathering themselves together at a central point, the surfaces of these globes lay in great fissures and yawning abysses. Nowhere are they smooth and even, as the body of the sun. These worlds are not destined to be suns, but *worlds that are at length to be inhabited by Man.* In their present state, they have neither water nor atmosphere.

The earth globe has a substance that is all alike, something as the substance of an apple appears all alike. It is soft and uneven, without water or atmosphere, turning on its own axis once in 24 hours. *The sun's warmth and attractive power causes it to describe a certain pathway or orbit of its own.*

As earlier stated, the sun has no atmosphere and the globe has no atmosphere. The heat of the sun strikes the globe without any modification whatever. Its rays are hotter than red heat. Consequently, the globe commences to bake and harden through and through.

As this globe bakes and gradually hardens in the scorching rays of the sun, every particle of water is baked or squeezed out of each atom. Every part is baked through, evenly and alike. There being no atmosphere, the water does not rise but runs down into all the fissures and chasms. The solid parts of the atom all become solid rock, baked like clay in a potter's oven, but the magnetic flame of each atom still remains within each atom. *It is only the fluid which is squeezed out, or the water, and the spirit of each atom is still within it.*

Now the globe is a solid mass of rock and water, but the water is principally on or near the surface of the globe so that she appears to be composed of vast bodies of water and comparatively smaller bodies of rock, yet her water is only one third of her bulk and only appears otherwise because it lies mostly upon her surface.

The ethereal and germinal sea remain intact. This globe is actually rolling within the ethereal and germinal sea. At this point of her career, *she is bathed in pure magnetism as it passes from the sun's magnetic counterpart and she is bathed in the light and heat from the sun as it passes to its magnetic counterpart.*

Now atmospheric air must be evolved. **All nature is evolved or separated, one thing from another.** Atmospheric air is one of the constituents of the water. Each drop of water is one third air. The air and the water must now be separated.

The water is lying smooth and glassy all over the earth in vast bodies, the hot and jagged rocks rising up from it in sterile grandeur. There are no winds to move the water or to cool the rock, no atmosphere to shield the earth from the awful heat.

The water is, at length, heated to the degree that the air is squeezed out of it. It commences to boil and bubble through all its vastness. **The terrible heat is causing it to yield up its air.** There is nothing to hinder the heat from penetrating to its remotest depths.

Now the globe is surrounded by hot steam or vapor. The waters keep on bubbling and boiling and throwing off hot air until the globe is surrounded by the hot vapor to a thickness of three miles or more.

Here is an earth composed of rock, water and air or hot vapor. It is a compound of genuine air and water, for the air in escaping carries a portion of the water along with it. But the water, being heavier than the air, gradually condenses and falls back to the earth in the form of rain which continually washes away at the hot rocks.

Water in and of itself is cold in its nature. It is only the unmitigated rays of the blazing sun that have caused this heated state of things. The water gradually cools the heated rock and for ages it washes away until it forms channels and rivers in the sides of the rocks and thus gradually washes and grinds the rocks into powder.

After an atmosphere has formed about the earth, *the motion of the earth is more rapid than the atmosphere. This causes immense currents of terrible winds to blow. The winds, disturbing the magnetic and electric currents that are passing to and from the sun and its counterpart, strike as lightning* upon the rocks, rending them asunder and splitting them into fragments and fissures, casting them right and left, hurling immense boulders of rock here, there and everywhere. All destined eventually to bring about a more perfect and equal state of things.

The earth is now at that point in its career where it is composed of rock, water and atmosphere. As yet, there is no ocean. The waters all lay in the deep fissures and chasms of the earth. The water was all heated to boiling and there were terrible winds, great whirlwinds and forked lightning constantly splitting the rocks asunder. The waters were constantly lashed into dreadful fury which gradually grinds and powders the rocks.

The rocks are so leveled in places that the oceans are formed by the water gathering into the places leveled. The rocks are powdered by all the rivers and streams cutting their way through to more level oceans, for all things seek their level. The waters carry along the powdered rock which is composed of minerals and sand. The minerals, by the common law of attraction, settle by themselves in beds, but all things that are soluble in water, the waters keep, *for these eventually form fish—-the first and lowest form of life.* Ages must pass before life can make its appearance, even in the ocean. *It is in the ocean that life first makes its appearance. The sponge and jellyfish are the first forms that material life takes on,* and even this cannot be until the waters become cool enough for them to exist.

The waters at length become comparatively cool and the atmosphere is somewhat cooler. *It is the shielding atmosphere which enables the waters to become cool.*

As the earth grows older and more perfect, it recedes farther and farther away from the sun. The ocean is gradually and constantly changing its bed, owing to it's rotary motion. At length, the atmosphere becomes cool enough for moss to grow upon the rocks and then small ferns. At the same time, the ocean and the waters become alive with fish of all kinds.

As soon as moss can form upon the rocks it is formed in this way, or primary primitive moss was, and can be observed today as well as any time, for it is always forming where the surface of a rock has decayed in the slightest.

Tiny scales of rock raise themselves up a little from the surface, something in the form of irregular leaves. The little flame of magnetic attraction has not left the atoms composing the earth, which at this period of history is all rocks. *It attracts and holds the lowest form of germ, or moss germ which is within the ethereal sea* and thus, moss grows as rapidly as time and seasons will allow. *All germs are within the atmosphere.* The ethereal sea and the germinal sea within it are left intact. The earth's atmosphere, made up of dense atmosphere, ethereal atmosphere and germinal points, does not displace the ethereal or the germinal sea.

Sponge within the sea is formed the same way but more rapidly, for it commenced on the wet rocks and there gathers sustenance from the sea. The germ of the living sponge is attracted in the same way from out of the ethereal sea or from out of the atmosphere. The germs of all things that live and grow are within the ethereal atmosphere and are invisible.

As soon as there is gelatin enough within the waters from dead and decaying sponge, it is washed here and there into little jelly-like masses. This higher form attracts and holds the higher germ of the jellyfish.

The jellyfish within the warm waters grows to an enormous size. Its substance, by the constant washing of the water, becomes separated into the form of long arms or legs, something like spiders. There you have the ocean tarantula that still keeps up the same motion as the jellyfish, which it really is. Its long arms wind about and draw in everything within its reach.

As the jellyfish grows and becomes old, the arms drop off. The living principle still resides within them. These form great water serpents and enormous eels which love to wallow in the bed of the ocean. They suck their sustenance partly from the water and partly from the decomposed rock. At the same time, the rocks that are not within the waters are forming moss. Then within the moss springs up small ferns. When these decay, they, in the moist warm rains, become gelatinous and **in this form attract and hold the lowest germs of animal or insect life.** They become enormous, soft, pale yellow spiders or tarantulas.

The arms or legs at last become so large they are broken or thrown off, but still retain the life within them. They become great serpents. These crawl about over the rocks, hiding in the fissures and chasms, sucking at the decaying mosses and ferns, growing and increasing in size. The great sea serpents crawl up on the sands of the beach and bask a part of their huge bodies in the rays of the sun which hardens them, or the part of them which is out of the water.

As the sun hardens them, it also changes their color from the color of a jellyfish to a darker hue. Many of them become something like enormous alligators without tongue or teeth. They merely have the power of sucking, yet their food is still within the sea.

At the same time, some of the great serpents on rock, for there is not any soil at this period, become lizards. These things are forming today just the same, modified by the cooler atmosphere.

At length, from the continual motion of the water, the rocks and sand become so powdered that seaweed and grasses appear. On the land, the mouldering mosses and ferns form very thin soil, perhaps an inch or two in thickness. This brings forth the fine, low grasses: something like the buffalo grass. The mountain bluegrass and buffalo grass are fair examples of this primitive grass. They are forming today, just as much as ever they were, with modification.

The oceans and all the rivers and streams are constantly changing their beds. As the oceans recede and change their beds, the immense quantities of seaweed, powdered rock, decaying jellyfish, eels and serpents form a deep alluvial soil. Out of this spring up giant ferns, weeds and various kinds of rank tropical vegetation.

Great marshes and swamps come to be from the exceedingly rapid growth of this coarse vegetation and are swarmed with giant snakes, eels, primitive alligators and, at length, huge whales come to be. As the ocean recedes, the swamps are gradually drained. The rank, decaying vegetation keeps on forming bed after bed of deep, rich soil. Then spring up magnificent forests of palm and other kinds of trees.

As yet, there has been no fire on the earth. The atmosphere is too warm, moist and thick with vapors. Birds have not yet come to be; nothing but the lowest form of animal and reptile life have come to be.

As the ocean recedes, it leaves sandy deserts. Now a period is reached in the earth's career where it is made up of great rocky mountains, sandy deserts, interminable marshes and tangled forests seemingly without end.

The oceans keep up a continual encroachment upon the mountains one way, leaving great marshes and sandy deserts the other way. After ages pass, the places where the highest peaks of mountains had been, will, at length, become the bed of the waters. *Thus it is that soil, vegetation, low animal life and the most primitive form of birds first come into being.*

The first form of a flying insect is a mosquito. They are of an enormous size, inhabiting the marshes. Then, maggots form within the decaying offshoot of the jellyfish that are left on the shores, for these creatures hold life within every part of them. Each germinal point becomes a maggot. *The maggots become great flies.* Now, we have the mosquito and the fly of enormous size and, at length, *from the mosquito, springs a creature something like a stork.* These are soft, huge things that can just flap their wings and jump from log to log or mound to mound and dive their great, soft bills into the waters and fish out a wriggling eel or a water snake which they immediately suck down into a great maw.

When each creature's maw is full, it will go and perch high up, away from the water for fear the wriggling things will escape, for life will not become extinct with them for some days. The great thing will sit stupidly for weeks until its maw is empty and its food has been digested. It then will descend and drink its fill of fresh water. It will repeat the process over again. *From the flies, at length, come great buzzards* that are not far removed from the primitive stork.

Many of these creatures live for hundreds of years: the whale and the stork and many of the great serpents. As the creatures wander or are left by the tide out on the sandy deserts and plains, their natures gradually become changed. By the action of the sun, they become hardened. *All these lowest creatures hold the female and male element within each one.*

They have not yet separated and become two distinct forms. The lowest forms of serpents have no lungs, they cannot breathe. They have no eyes, they cannot see.

Until a creature has developed a very small lung, *it cannot attract the germinal point from the atmosphere.* It draws its life as the jellyfish does. Neither has it any blood. Flies and mosquitoes develop a very small lung. Therefore, they can attract and hold germinal points. *These develop eggs.* Now the eggs can be laid and hatched. The stork scoops shallow holes in the hot sand with her long bill and deposits her eggs therein.

The fishes begin to spawn in the waters. But they are not like the fish of today, they are enormously large and of a soft, primitive kind that holds the male and female principles in one. The first form of crocodile life is the same. They lay their eggs in the hot sand. The sands are literally filled with them and, *as they hatch, the male and female principle takes a step in advance.*

They hatch equal numbers, male and female. That is, *each germinal point separates its male and female principles into two forms.* These forms that are hatched from the hot sands are smaller, harder and more perfect and have lungs developed as they grow and, consequently have red blood.

The spawn within the sea is the same: it hatches smaller and more fishes, male and female, with colder red blood. The lungs are in the form of large gills and gradually *a regular vertebrae and bones are formed.*

As time goes on, great elephants roam the forests and the plains. The mastodon wades in the swamp, the camel trods the hot sands. Then, the great lion and bear appear. The eagle the ostrich and the ape.

The earth is now cool enough for Man to make his appearance. Presently, from the highest form of ape walks forth a dark, hairy, squat savage with long arms. He carries a club and wields stones with which he kills birds, animals and serpents. He tears them in pieces with his long claws and teeth, devouring them fiercely with gleaming eyes, for **as lungs were developed, so were eyes.** Lungs, eyes and blood depend on atmosphere to sustain them…

This was the first form of Man that the earth ever knew.

HEAT & LIGHT

The Law of Soul Gravitation.

Mankind has never yet arrived at the true cause of light and heat of the sun.

The sun is not a single body as it appears to be, but **dual in it's nature**—just as man and woman, when once they become spiritualized and enter the angelic state, are dual and yet appear as one. The true halves were one from the beginning and were separated into two forms that they may take on material substance or a material body **for the purpose of propagation and progression.**

The sun was once a soft primary world and never inhabited. After it had cast off its children, which is our solar system it, at length, grew old and died or yielded up its spirit, which, like all other spirit, was pure magnetic flame. This flame could not again clothe itself with matter because all atoms **each hold themselves in their own magnetic flame.** They cannot be robbed. Therefore, **the pure magnetic flame, or spirit, must necessarily retain the form which it had left.** In passing from the body of the sun, the pure magnetic flame or spirit took a straight course. It became opposed, or lay in direct opposition to the sun, far removed and outside of the planets, always keeping itself directly opposite the sun. This globe, being purely magnetic or spiritual, is not visible to Man. The body of the sun which it had left was and is a coal-black mass of pure elementary carbon.

All the suns are dual in their nature, the real bodies of the two being composed of elementary principles: magnetism and carbon. *It is the play of these two elements back and forth which causes light and heat.*

Lightning is caused by the meeting of two elements. As they meet, one sets fire to the other and an explosion follows which gives the bright flash. The two elementary bodies of the sun act in precisely the same way. *As each one revolves, each throws off its elementary principle.* As these elements meet, one sets fire to the other and combustion is the result.

Nothing is ever seen of the sun but the *result* of these two forces. The blazing light is seen but not the two bodies of the sun itself.

Magnetism and carbon keep up an eternal play, and *it is the leaping of electricity from one globe to the other that is the true cause of light and heat.* The magnetic globe sends great waves of magnetism to the carbonic globe. This sets the carbon on fire and the electric rays dart straight back to the magnetic globe where they are again resolved into magnetism proper and are sent back to the carbonic globe.

The carbonic globe loses nothing. The magnetic globe loses nothing. Each forever feeds the other. It is merely give and take, give and take, and their children—*the planets—are nourished and fed between these two globes.* They are warmed and lighted by the electric rays as they dart straight on their course to the magnetic globe.

They are bathed in magnetism **which is not visible** as it rolls in majestic waves back to the carbonic globe.

Man does not see the black body of carbon. He does not see the pale amber globe of magnetism. But he does see the electric rays as they leap forth from the carbonic globe, and this to him is the sun. **It is but the electric light which he perceives. Therefore, he thinks there is but one sun.** He is mistaken.

The sun of our system of worlds is the only one that emits light and heat. The other planets have no light and heat of their own. They would not be visible to earth at all but for the light from the sun shining on them when a part of the earth is in darkness or shadow as that portion of it is turned away from the sun.

Unlike the earth, the sun is not an inhabited planet. It is not solid and compact like the earth and is composed of two distinct and separate bodies. It is now **spiritual or gaseous** in its nature and holds in solution all the elements. The light and heat of the sun is caused by the playing back and forth of the great eternal principles of which it's bodies are composed. **Call them carbon, magnetism, electricity, spirit and matter, gases, positive and negative forces, hydrogen, nitrogen, oxygen—anything and everything.**

One of the bodies of the sun is black as night, the other is a pale amber flame. **They lie millions of miles apart** but always directly opposite each other. They roll in their orbits exactly at the same rate. The black body is called carbon and the amber body is called magnetism.

The sun is a vast electric light. One being naturally a great chemical laboratory, the other the attractive power drawing all these elements to itself and thereby bursting into flaming light.

Suns are formed or grow within the limitless eternal sea of atoms.

The real bodies of the suns are not visible to Man, nor could they be owing to the blazing light which they generate. This light is really a burning, flaming light caused by combustion.

The motive power that causes the piston in the cylinder of a locomotive to work up and down, to move, to pulse or beat is **steam**. The cause of steam is boiling water. Boiling water is caused by heat. The cause of heat is ignition, which is caused by a spark of electricity.

Expansion causes water to rise into the atmosphere. Heat causes expansion. One can see the rising vapor, but not the heat. Heat is the motive power or vehicle which causes the water to rise. But even heat has not the power to take the water beyond a certain level when it must leave it. When heat has left it, the water condenses with cold and falls back to earth.

Heat rises. Air is not heat and air is not cold. **Heat and cold are distinct properties from air.** Heat and cold are merely the agents that move or displace air, just as they displace water. Water is not heat, neither is the air. Heat is a distinct property.

Combustion is the cause of heat. Combustion is caused by the uniting of two forces in nature: magnetism and carbon, both invisible to Man. They are elementary forces that exist throughout eternity. Heat is the result of the coalescing of these two great forces in nature. Heat is forever rushing to find its level and, as it rushes on, it carries a great many other things with it besides water and leaves them at their proper level just as it does water. **It also carries the spiritual or life forces within it** and leaves them at **their** proper level. It is a great winged vehicle, loaded with the most precious freight and always leaving all things in their rightful places or at their proper level. And it still rushes on.

Heat is the vehicle that carries a Man's spiritual body to its proper altitude and leaves it within the spiritual spheres for **heat goes with the spirit**, and does not remain with the material body. Heat is the coalescing of two great forces in nature: magnetism and carbon, and electricity or heat, is the result. **Heat is simply electricity** and electricity is an invisible force, as are also magnetism and carbon.

Electricity is the vehicle on which a Man's soul rises to its proper level. Electricity or heat is not an intelligent force. **Intelligence is the subtle power behind all this.**

The intelligent soul of Man holds magnetism in one hand, carbon in the other, and by the uniting of the two forces, rises on the wings of electricity.

His spiritual body is composed of magnetism and carbon and the electricity is the vehicle in which he rides. His will, or intelligence, holds together and governs these forces. An undeveloped intelligence exists in an invisible germinal point within the atmosphere. It was started on its journey through matter by its earthly parents. **It at length becomes developed intelligence.**

Each intelligence is distinct and separate from another intelligence. In other words, each soul is a distinct and unique soul. As this intelligence develops, it gathers to itself and holds, by the power of magnetic attraction, a material body. This material body obeys the growth or development of the intelligent soul.

As the soul exists as an invisible entity before it takes on matter, it must, of necessity, exist as a developed entity when it leaves matter behind. **On leaving matter, it takes heat or electricity with it as well as the magnetism which holds the body together; for the body, when the intelligent soul has left it and taken heat and magnetism with it, falls apart.**

39

The developed intelligence carries heat and magnetism with it because it **need**s them. Heat is invisible, magnetism is invisible and intelligence is invisible.

The intelligent soul of Man governs that which creates his own body. Spiritual body is composed of magnetism and electricity *and is held together by the intelligent soul.*

Magnetism and heat or electricity and intelligence are all invisible and are indestructible. This amply proves the immortality of Man.

He rises on the wings of electricity or heat and governs that which constitutes his own body to suit himself. He can move by the power of his will or intelligence—move his magnetic and electric body wherever he will. *Electricity is his vehicle and magnetism the clothing of his soul or his intelligence.*

The developed intelligent soul is clothed in a pale magnetic flame. Electricity is its weapon or vice-regent, the agent by which it moves and accomplishes its will. Such a soul or intelligence or many intelligences may or can, if they so desire, wield their electric weapons accordingly as they will.

They can gather to themselves a heavy or a light magnetic clothing at their will, and when they are at their own proper level within the spiritual spheres, their magnetic bodies are quite dense and palpable. But when they travel by the aid of their electrical powers and visit earth or other planets, *they must leave behind or cast off much of this dense magnetic body or it impedes their flight.* They can take it on again at pleasure. They are palpable and visible to each other but not to the human eye.

All natural objects exist above as they do on earth and draw to themselves their own covering of sublimated matter. *All matter is chemical in its nature. The sun dissolves all material things as rapidly as possible and draws them upward into the celestial world.*

Water, gases, carbon and all chemical properties are drawn up by the sun in countless millions and billions of tons. Not only are *they* drawn upward or outward, but *all material things which first existed as elementary or chemical properties within the never ending ether are as well.*

There is nothing new, neither within the heavens nor upon the earth. Everything is as old as eternity itself. Everything always has existed and always will. The sun existed before it became a body of light, but it existed in the form of atoms. All eternity is composed of the male and female principles, positive and negative, spirit and matter. *The very lowest, first forms in existence, have the two principles combined in one form.* This is also true of the atoms. Each atom is a tiny speck of pure flame, or spirit or magnetism, surrounded and covered by matter. *The spirit within the heart of the atom is the female principle; that which covers and conceals it is the male principle.* These can be called by any other names: force and matter, potentialities and so forth, but male and female principles, positive and negative more exactly express the truth.

The law of magnetic attraction is to hold or grasp each atom as closely as possible, and soon a body, or small globe is formed. *This is what we denominate "growth" within the eternal sea of atoms.* Countless suns are forming or growing at all times. They ever have been and ever will be. As this small globe of atoms revolves, it continually attracts and holds other atoms and all atoms that are anywhere within its attractive power. It's size, together with its orbit, constantly increases and all eternity is before it. It has no need of hurry.

Our Creator is "He" and "She", forever at oneness in nature. Nature in all her varied methods never evolves into one great hybrid—male nor female. Neither is sex a matter of accident but a great eternal law in nature. Every atom in the universe is male *and* female, united in oneness at the very foundation of all that exists. **Without the two principles in equal proportion, nothing can exist or be created—it is Creation itself, or Creator.**

If the light and heat of the sun was simply caused by vibratory action, all the planets together with the earth would be suns of more or less magnitude. Such is not the case. The planets simply shine with reflected light. *That is, they reflect the light of the sun which is shining upon them, and all these reflected rays are again returned to the sun to be observed within her vast laboratory where they return to their former chemical condition.* Again they are sent forth in great magnetic waves to the black body or the counterpart, once again bursting forth into blazing glory, then again darting through space to warm and vivify the planets together with the moons which the planets have thrown off.

The moon is not an old and worn out world, but a baby world not yet fit for habitation. The moons of Jupiter and Saturn are not old worn out worlds. They have been thrown off from those planets, they are their children.

All nature moves in circles or families, with father, mother and children, or positive and negative principles producing a third form, and thereafter many forms.

The elementary principles exist first. They take form within the material and those forms then give up their spirit so that they can then exist as forms within the spheres of the ethereal or celestial world.

The spiritual world is not composed of spheres alone, but exists within all space and distances between the globes or spheres of more material matter. There are planes and never ending planes of existing things. There is room enough and time enough throughout eternity for all to live, for all to grow, for all to become wise, for all eventually to be gods in their own right and in their own way.

All spiritual forms arise up and away from the material but before rising, they often make themselves both seen and felt. A dying rose, as it arises from the material, is materially sensed by its perfume which is really the spiritual substance of the rose arising on its way to fairer climes.

Again, all things are immortal. Life is spirit and spirit is immortal in whatever form it may exist. The tiniest blade of grass is just as immortal as is Man. No form, when once attained, is ever resolved back into elementary principles. Matter falls away from it, but the *form* is retained forever.

As matter falls away from the spiritual forms of humanity, it falls away from all other forms in precisely the same way, leaving the spiritual form intact. The life of anything is its spiritual form more or less developed. *All things have their roots in material earths.*

The spiritual world is real and tangible but exquisitely fine, more beautiful than the earthly world. It is composed of the quintessence of all things that belong to earth. *These things get there mostly on the wings of heat.*

Water is not the only thing that heat carries upward or outward away from earth. *It is carrying everything that belongs to earth in the same way.*

On a bright, sunny day, especially if it is hot, many flowers wither and die. Heat is bearing them away to the spiritual realm. Much, but not all of the water that is carried up, returns to earth. A portion becomes too rare and never returns. This forms the rare and expanded water of the spiritual spheres. All this water rises and the greater part of it is carried up on the brightest and sunniest days.

One cannot see the essence of spirit of all that appears to die on earth as it is carried by heat outward or upward into the spirit realms. The spiritual earth or ground is the aggregation of chemical vapors that arise from material earth and, through the great law of chemical affinity, coalesce into ethereal spiritual lands or spiritual ground. Nothing there grows from seeds. Seeds do not germinate anywhere but on the material earths and *earths nourish the spiritual.*

From the atmosphere, Man inhales the germs of life: **the germs which are to be the living souls of the next generation.** *Protoplasm or matter has no life whatever of its own and the life principle does not reside within it.* When that cell of protoplasm is exposed to the air, it attracts from the atmosphere a germ of life, a spiritual germ. The germ begins to expand, grow, evolve. First involution, then evolution.

Taking the law of evolution in one hand and the law of involution in the other, the road to immortality is made plain and easy. If you discover one law, you must find its counterpart: male and female, positive and negative, involution and evolution. Every existing law has its counterpart: heaven and earth, spirit and matter and so forth. If the higher did not assist the lower in all things, creation would be at a standstill. Chaos would result.

The very lowest forms of life are various species of moss upon the rocks and the living, gelatinous masses found in the seas. Rocks decay slightly. *The decayed matter of the rocks and the moisture of the air or rain makes protoplasm, the germ of moss, which resides within the atmosphere.*

The spirit, or living germ, buries itself within the protoplasm, covers itself with it. Otherwise the germ could never develop into that which nature designed it to be: *the first or lowest life upon the earth.*

When the moss decays or dies, the life or spirit of it ascends as developed spiritual moss into the ethereal atmosphere or celestial world to beautify the celestial spheres. *The matter or protoplasm remains on earth* and, after many accumulations, becomes soil fitted for higher germs of vegetation. As fast as the higher germs find suitable soil or matter wherein to hide, higher and still higher forms of vegetation appear until, through the laws of involution and evolution, vegetation arrives at that point where a tiny flower appears.

The flower holds the attractive force and gathers within its tiny cup the spiritual germ and holds it fast until seed is formed. Now involution and evolution have given us seed.

By involution, a higher state of things has been evolved until insect and animal life is arrived at. A point is reached when the great laws of involution and evolution take on the form of male and female.

Each male form now inhales and holds the spiritual germ of the future generation. The same principle applies to all life within the waters. All life originates within the atmosphere, or ether. It all returns to it again developed and beautified, *that is the sole object of spirit and matter, or ethereal germs and protoplasm.*

Nothing propagates itself in the spiritual world. There is growth and progression but not propagation. The material earths are the only places where propagation takes place. *All spiritual things have their root in the material.*

The spirit of all things that die on earth pass directly to *that* earth's spiritual spheres and take their places according to natural law. *That is the true meaning of all death.*

Animals have a right to exist on a spiritual level like humans. Animals are just as beautiful in their way as human beings. They are not so intelligent but just as necessary in the chain of existent things as either you or I. The germs of eternal truth are lying dormant within every spiritual being that exists. There is a law of soul gravitation just as there is a law of material gravitation.

Light and heat create the spiritual world. Nothing does die. It simply changes that a higher state of being might exist. Light and heat are the vehicles on which the spiritual travels to its destination.

Spiritual water is brought hither by heat: light unloaded it and placed it where it belongs. All water above the earth has been carried there from the earth. Heat works silently. Heat performs wonderful feats. If it were not for heat's enemy, cold, heat would dissolve the earth in a short time and carry it all away. But the burdened army of heat must fight it's way through the dense army of cold which robs a large portion of it.

If this were not so, not one drop of water which heat had taken up would ever fall back to earth. Cold has not the power to rob heat of all it's hidden treasures, a portion is still left and these are deposited at the feet of light. Heat carries water up. Cold condenses or robs heat of a larger portion of itself. Cold merely robs heat of the heavier, coarser parts of which water is composed. It leaves the refined essence of water within the spiritual realm and the color rays of light place it where it belongs. Thus are the waters of the spiritual world gathered together.

The same vehicle which brings water to the spiritual, brings the flowers and foliage. When a flower yields up its perfume, or life on earth, it is carried upward that one's nostrils are able to perceive it. It is carried by heat and **the perfume never returns after it has once ascended.** Heat never yields up his treasure, for it belongs to the soul of the flower. The largest portion of the water which enters into the composition of the flower is condensed and carried back by cold, but it's inner essences heat deposits in the spiritual world. Light and color rays claim their own. The form, the beauty and inner essence of the flower remain forever undestroyed.

Earth keeps back the dull, outer husk that the flower no longer needs which would only detract from and mar it's beauty. Thus the spiritual world of trees, foliage and flowers are brought together. So it is with birds, beasts and Man: *the soul, the form, the inner essence are all carried upward by heat. Cold condenses and returns to earth all that is coarse and heavy.* The sweetest and most precious treasures are carried by heat beyond the atmosphere of earth, beyond the cold and deposited by light. With it's pencil rays of exquisite colors in great spiritual zones about the earth, they rest within the spiritual ether: worlds upon worlds of exquisite life and beauty!

Man thinks there is nothing between him and the sun but clear atmosphere. When the light of the sun is obscured by the earth's shadow at night, Man looks into the same atmosphere and there are thousands of worlds revealed to his sight. Still he thinks there is nothing between him and the moon and stars but the atmosphere and space: interstellar space.

The bright material light of the sun hides from Man's sight in the daytime all of the spiritual zones or worlds which lie between the earth and the stars. It also hides the stars. At night, darkness hides the spiritual zones or worlds from Man's sight. He can see nothing but the material light of the moon and stars, which does not reveal the refined and spiritual which lie between.

Exquisite coloring resides within light and when conditions are favorable and one can see a rainbow, that fact is revealed. Light is made up of different colored rays. Each ray is chemical in its nature, and each ray can be robbed of a portion of its chemical coloring: matter. Rays of light may be called white, for unless they are colored by chemical compounds, every ray would be white. As each ray is colored, and there are many different shades of color, the white rays are transformed into all the colors of the rainbow.

Heat has set the canvas and forms drawn therein. That is, heat has brought upward attenuated matter in all its various forms. Attenuated matter might be likened unto loose canvas, with the forms of all things outlined within its meshes. For instance, heat has set the ethereal or volatile essence of a rose or any other flower or leaf and that ethereal essence retains the form it wore on earth. The color rays commence to rob heat of its treasure through chemical assimilation. The attenuated ethereal essence attracts and holds the chemical dyes that are in the color rays. The more dense the essence, the lower the spiritual strata. Heat retains a finer, more ethereal essence still, together with more shadowy forms, and this again attracts finer, more perfect shading, and a higher spiritual sphere is formed. All these things rise, sphere upon sphere unnumbered, each finer than the last. The earth has been yielding up its treasures for countless ages, and countless millions of souls dwell upon the spheres. Eternity stretches onward, upward, downward, and forever and ever.

Attenuated matter, or the volatile essence of all things that die on earth, chemically unites with the color rays of light by natural selection or affinity. When thus united, they form the spiritual zones or spheres. The soul of Man also rises on the wings of heat, carrying his ethereal essences with him. After chemical coalescence with the color rays of light, Man takes his proper place within the heavenly spheres.

Water evolves air, air ether, the earth evolves spiritual essences, and all living things evolve spiritual life...

THE SPIRIT OF
ALL THINGS

The magnetic flame within.

The spirit of an atom is the little magnetic flame within each atom. The spirit within all the earth is magnetism, as the spirit of the sun is magnetism. The body of the sun was obliged to yield up its spirit before it could be a sun, and now the earth must gradually yield up its spirit.

The earth commences a step farther on in the scale of progress than does the sun. The sun is a primary world, the earth a secondary world. *Spirit, in and of itself is not intelligent. It is pure magnetism.* The moment a particle of rock is softened enough to attract a moss germ, and the spiritual germs of moss have developed into the form of moss, as soon as that moss decays or yields up its magnetic flame, *a spiritual sphere is commenced.*

About the moon: The earth has yielded up just so much of its magnetism; and so of everything else that exists or develops upon the earth. At this period of the earth's history there is no moon, for the moon is an offshoot, or ring, cast off from the earth. The following is the way in which the moon is gradually formed:

A germ, in developing, uses up about **one third** of the magnetism composing its entire material substance. When it rises up in its spiritual form, **two-thirds** of the magnetism which has entered into the composition of its material form is left behind. **These atoms remain on earth to be worked up into some other form.** But **one third** of the atoms left behind have given up their magnetism and have become worthless or worn out. The magnetic spirit has gone out of them and now exists in a form which covers the developed germ. These worthless atoms, which have lost their magnetic flame, now have no power of attraction or of being attracted. They lie helpless at the mercy of the atmosphere. They rise to the surface of the atmosphere and there remain in helpless masses.

As fast as the magnetic spiritual sphere is formed which, in forming, has robbed some atoms of their spirit, this ring or belt of worthless atoms thickens and increases and, as the ages roll on, becomes very large and heavy.

There is a way in which the worthless atoms are replenished and again filled with spirit or magnetic flame: **comets are great wandering torches of magnetic flame or pure magnetism.** In other words, **they are spirit devoid of matter.** These great magnetic torches visit the planets and revivify the worthless or worn out atoms that rise up and surround the planet. When each atom has received its just amount of magnetic flame, it is just as good as ever. It can now attract and be attracted so it attaches itself together in the form of a compact ring such as the rings around the planet Saturn.

Before the worthless atoms are revivified, they appear as vast belts. After they are revivified and welded together by the attraction of magnetic spirit, they appear as a vast ring. At length this ring has become large and heavy. It breaks in pieces and falls away from the parent globe, gathers itself together at its central point, *and there is a moon!*

About this period in earth time, Man became observing and intelligent. Ages upon ages have passed since then; empires and great cities have had their rise and fall and Man is at his present altitude.

A new era is about to dawn upon the world. Man has had no very clear vision of his future. The time is now coming when he is to know just how his life is to be in the future. In order to understand the future, one must understand the past. *All nature has toiled together for countless ages to bring forth an intelligent soul. All things work together for this one object. The germ of Man within the germinal sea is the highest germ there is. From this germ comes forth the angel!*

All other things in nature are merely to serve Man, to develop and bring him forth. He comes last, for all that is lower must exist that he may have a home and foothold wherein to develop into an angel. All things beneath him must yield up their spiritual form that he may have a spiritual home at last within the ethereal sea which has been robbed of its germs that they may be developed into this higher form.

It is better to be an angel far on the road toward wisdom, love, and happiness than to be an invisible germinal point without intelligence within the ethereal sea...

Imagining if looking through a spiritual microscope, one could see a spiritual germ, the germ of a Man not yet incarnated. It looks like a little ethereal globe, transparent and translucent. Within the globe are two forms, perfect in every respect, with this difference: one is male and the other female. They are exact counterparts of each other: this is the undeveloped germ of a Man or of an angel yet to be. No two globes are alike. They differ as much as people do on earth. No two germs are alike any more than two people, for they, at length, *are* people and within each germ are two forms: male and female. They are one, ***the germ of an undivided angel.*** They belong to each other by a law, the law of soulmates, or counterparts. They exist as one within the spiritual germ, to be united again in oneness to their eternal counterparts in the spiritual realm, forming a complete angel. This is true of all angels that are or ever shall be.

The soul is composed of pure divine fire. The spark from the eternal ocean of divine life, the little globe of divine fire, the germ which is breathed in by Man becomes a living human being, or two living human beings, but not by the same parents. This germ, or spark, or translucent globe of pure soul fire is positive and negative and its nature is male and female. The divine life is not male, or "he", but "male" ***and*** "female", he ***and*** she, and the "he" and "she" are one in the divine life.

These divine or pure germs are not spirit, but ***soul.*** Soul is life and life is soul. An atom is composed of a point of pure spirit or magnetism which draws ***to*** itself. It covers itself with an equal amount of matter. It is formed like an egg, an egg so minute that it is not visible to the naked eye. The matter surrounds the spirit, or magnetism, and together they form the atom. But the germ of life, the soul-germ, is not there. That remains and resides within the ether, ***waiting until conditions are right*** for it to enter earthly substance wherein it develops into that which it is designed to be.

Matter, spirit, and soul form all the universes that exist forever and ever. Matter and spirit are merely the clothing for the soul or the life. ***Spirit is not life, neither is matter.*** Life is not, at first, within either until it, the soul germ, enters or is attracted when the proper time comes for it to do so.

When one is in the body of flesh, one is soul, spirit and matter, spirit and matter being the clothing of the soul. As this soul germ develops, it throws off matter but takes spirit along with it into the spiritual realm. *The spiritual realm is composed of the spirits of all things that have held life or a living germ. Consequently, life is immortal. It never had a beginning and never had an end, but it possesses the power of development.* If the soul germ, from having no beginning nor ending, enters matter and spirit for the purpose of development, simply casting aside its outer covering as it grows, immortality is a self-evident fact.

These germs, when they are born into the flesh, *are necessarily divided. For if they were not born on earth in two forms, male and female, propagation would be at an end.* Angels do not propagate. Therefore, these divided halves are later joined again in the spheres in order to make the complete angel, yet they are still in two forms as within the germ.

The half of one germ cannot fit or be the actual half of another germ. One may take a bushel of apples and cut them all in half. Unless he gets the real half of each apple that was cut, he might put an apple together whose halves did not belong to the same apple.

When Man breathes in this globe or germ by a natural process it, during the process, separates. The positive or negative half, as the case may be, becoming a sperm. The other half is thrown back into the ether or air to be inhaled by some other male and incarnated as soon as may be. The half that is thrown out or exhaled, is not now a perfect globe, being but half. It takes on an oblong form, consequently remaining close to the earth, thereby becoming incarnated more quickly than a perfect or whole spark or germ. These are born into earth life, male and female, by different parents. One father and mother begats the male and one father and mother begats the female. One is a boy the other a girl, but in the soul germ, or divine globe fire, they were one. As angels, or perfected souls in the spheres, they will become one again. This is unalterable and unchangeable. Not a creature ever born on earth could change it.

As it now is, it matters not how many wives a man may marry or how many women he may unite himself to, his soul is never satisfied. He never ceases to feel that secret longing and yearning for a love which he has not until he finds the one that was his companion within the little spiritual germ. He must do this before he can become an angel. Before he is so united, he is not a completed angel but a wandering spirit.

It does not matter whether the two halves meet on earth. **The law of soulmates does not pertain to earth at all.** The separation of the positive and negative portions of the divine fire globe, or germ, **is for the purpose of propagation,** that children may have a father and mother for their short period of earthly life. Whether they meet or not is unimportant considering the eons of ages of immortality and eternity. Husband and wife who dearly love each other on earth might, even in the spheres, go on for a length of time together but the **separation would inevitably come if they were not soulmates.** Earthly marriages are for a time. Soulmates are for eternity. Earthly marriages are for the earth and should be kept inviolate, the husband as pure and true as the wife. No pure wife should live with an impure husband and vice versa. Each husband and wife should live true and pure to one another, seeking no affinities, nor even soulmates, for **this is not of the earth but for the heavens.**

Throughout eternity when one finds his companion that was within the spiritual germ, he or she calls that one 'wife' or 'husband'.

There is no desire to call any other person 'wife' or 'husband'. Even the thought of such a thing, if it were possible, would bring pandemonium instead of heaven. The great unchangeable laws of nature provide for all things. If the germs were not male and female in one, there might be more males than females or the reverse. There could be no harmony or happiness if such had to live without their corresponding half or, if some had to live as females without a male forever or the reverse. That would be living as halves and not a complete whole, while others would be complete. The halves would have great reason to complain of injustice. But nature is not haphazard like this.

The earth is surrounded by spiritual and angelic spheres. *The spirits of all things ascend, even the spirits of moss and grass.* The spirit of all things is the magnetic flame within. *That magnetic flame is the clothing of the developed germ,* the spiritual or soul germ which matter attracts to itself from out of the ethereal atmosphere. It is the magnetic flame within each atom which attracts the germ *as soon as matter is in a suitable state to receive and hold these things. The germ is the living principle within all things; without it, all other things would be dead or inert.* These germs only wait for suitable material in order to enter it, then develop as rapidly as possible.

This is the answer to "what is that life within all things?" *It is one of these germinal points which is developing and growing up through matter and covering itself with matter until it has attained its full size and form, after its own kind and species.* As soon as it has attained its ultimate or perfect form, it begins to throw off its coarser covering of matter but retains or holds to itself as much of the magnetic flame as it needs for a spiritual covering. It then rises from the earth in its developed and beautiful spiritual form.

According to natural law, it now takes its place within one of the spiritual spheres which surround the globe or planet or earth. ***This is true of all life from the simple moss to the wisest Man that ever lived.***

The foundation of the first spiritual sphere of this earth is firmly laid within the upper strata of the earth's dense atmosphere, rising just as cream rises upon milk. The earth's atmosphere may be compared to milk that holds within it the essence of all things ***that to us seem to die:*** for instance, a flower or shrub of any kind slowly exhales its life and beauty. While it is giving up its essence, or spirit, we smell or sense it in the air. It is rising, going forth, rising to the surface of the dense atmosphere, for it is more ethereal in its nature. As fast as it exhales, or dies on earth it grows within the spiritual sphere. It gathers up all its sweet life, beauty and impalpable essence and becomes a flower, tree or shrub within the spiritual sphere: imperishable and immortal.

The same is true of all insects, reptiles, or animal life.

As for animals that eat other animals, the animal doesn't eat the spirit of the other animal, he cannot. The animal cannot catch the spirit and only eats the material part that is the fleshy body.

Man also dies on earth and his spirit ascends to this beautiful realm already prepared for him. He takes his place naturally within this world of life and beauty. There he creates houses, halls of learning and temples of wisdom from his artistic soul. Man cannot see each particle as it rises, no more than he can within milk. So the spiritual world is richer, firmer and more enduring than the thin air through which it rises.

There is a substantial world made up of the refined essences of all earthly material things. These ethereal essences rise up through the earth's atmosphere; that the soul of all things, ***which is the invisible*** *developed germ,* precedes or rises first and then draws or attracts a substantial material/spiritual covering. The soul of Man acts in the same manner. His soul, or invisible developed germ, rises. He attracts and draws to himself a substantial material/spiritual covering. He walks, talks and appears within that world very much as he does on earth except that he is the refined essence of the grosser, heavier, material earthly matter.

His soul can return and hold communication with Man on earth. As he does so, he leaves his refined material body behind him in the spiritual world. If the real spiritual body could return to earth, it would be as distinctly visible to Man as his mortal body. But *the soul, without its covering, is invisible.*

Ages before Man reached an intelligent altitude, these spiritual spheres had been forming. *This is the true meaning of all which is called "death". There is no such thing as death: it is merely the rising up of the perfectly developed germ with its proper amount of magnetic clothing and the leaving behind it of a coarser matter which it no longer needs.*

Within the spiritual and angelic spheres, there is all that one has on earth and there is all that the earth has ever produced. Earth is but the nucleus of vast spheres which surround it. These spheres are peopled with spirits, angels and spiritual forms of all things that ever had life with all the developed germs which the earth has been able to develop.

These spheres are so vast and grand that they are able to hold *in their proper place, in order,* all these variously developed forms. *Every year which the earth counts gives just so many more forms into the spheres; just so many more spirits and angels; just so many more worthless atoms rise up to eventually make another moon. This is true of all earths or secondary worlds that are not suns.*

Planets are secondary worlds, or inhabited worlds, that are yielding up their spirits very gradually and which go to make up the spiritual spheres.

There are at the present time ten thousand times ten thousand more angels within the heavenly spheres surrounding the earth than there are men upon the earth. These heavens have long been, and are still becoming, most wise and powerful. Every Man, woman and child on the earth is continually receiving visits from these angels, and are more or less aided and guided by them. Many men and women are conscious of their presence. There is a time in the distant future when all men will be so refined and spiritual that angels will be recognized companions by day and by night.

If the angels within the heavens had no loved ones on earth, not one of them would ever return. There are millions of angels that never do return to earth. It is this connecting link of love that draws earth up toward heaven and heaven down toward earth. *Love joins the two worlds together.*

Every blade of grass that ever grew on the earth, every flower, every shrub, every tree, every form that ever is developed on the earth, the spirit of that form exists within the spiritual spheres, more beautiful and more perfect, without a sign of death or decay. Animals live in heaven just as much as they do on earth. *Earth exists merely to create and populate heaven—for this and this alone.*

The heavenly spheres are so vast that they can and do contain all the life that the earth has ever yielded up. The spheres are constantly increasing and enlarging as earth yields up its spirit, year after year, season after season and as the spirits of countless millions of human beings also ascend to fill and enjoy them. There, animals and insects do not bite or sting, *because their bodies do not need to be sustained by material substance.* It is the spirit or form, and not the material body, that lives. These creatures enjoy their existence as much as Man enjoys his.

Nothing propagates on the spheres. There is nothing within all the heavenly spheres belonging to earth except those things that have been developed up and through matter on the earth. All that is on the spheres is but the spirit of those things which once existed on the earth. There is no propagation of any kind within any of the heavenly spheres. Earth can never furnish more than will perfect the heavens.

The earth is a secondary world and is yielding up its spirit through its countless forms of life, and thus forming the spiritual heavens for the happiness and form of Man, its crown or culmination, which is at last the all wise Godlike angel.

All living things first exist as spiritual germinal points swimming within the ethereal sea. As each germ is developed up through matter into its perfect form, it takes its proper place within the spiritual realm *there to exist forever.*

Spirits and angels can influence the spirit and body of mankind. A spirit or an angel can descend from its home within the heavens and mingle with a spirit that yet inhabits a material body. Angels can cast their light, their wisdom, and their truth down upon the spirits of men. And Man can see to walk in light. A galaxy of angels swings within their orbits of light that Man may raise his mind upward and light from the angels can penetrate his darkness.

Truth is entirely natural, for nature is truth. The first duty and mission of an angel is to discover truth and give it to the world. The angels highest mission is like the hour hand on the clock that moves slowly but surely toward the true time, pointing straight at truth.

Angels throw their rays of light and truth outward until they penetrate Man's ignorance and obtuseness. Spirits and angels in their higher and more perfect form can be with Man on earth because their forms are composed of ethereal substance and are filled with magnetism, which is an invisible flame. Their ethereal and magnetic bodies, coupled with their greater intelligence, are able to penetrate, fill and influence those still within a material body.

Atoms are composed of spirit in matter, or magnetism in matter. The marriage or union of spirit and matter brings forth form. The earths yield up their spiritual and angelic spheres, and people become spirits and angels. All things within the universe bear a relationship one to the other, that great analogous chain holds all things together.

The earth became rock and yielded up its water.

The water in its turn washed the rock.

The water yielded up its atmosphere.

The atmosphere in its turn embraced and kissed both rocks and water.

The atmosphere yielded up its ether, or ethereal atmosphere.

The ether in its turn permeated the atmosphere and the water and even the dark earth as much as possible.

All this was for the sole purpose of developing an imperishable, intelligent and at last an all wise angel.

A strict analogy runs through all things. Man yields up his spirit as the rock does the water. *The spirit in turn, purifies and enlightens Man.* Spirits yield up their higher principles, which is the angelic, and the angels embrace and kiss both spirits and Man. The angels become archangels and permeate and fill angels, spirits and Man with their wisdom.

Water can never return to its first condition before it was evolved from that which was at length to become rock.

The atmosphere can never again return and fill that which was water in its first form, and from which the air was evolved.

Ether can never again reside as an inseparable thing, or as one with air.

A spirit can never again return and be one with flesh and blood.

An angel can never return and be a spirit.

An archangel can never again be anything but an archangel, just as a Man can never again be a boy.

A boy can never again be a babe and a babe can never again be an undeveloped germ.

But the Man can instruct and guide the boy.

The boy can teach the babe to walk and the babe holds the undeveloped germ of the boy, Man, spirit, angel and archangel.

A full-grown tree can never again become a sapling.

A Man can never again become a babe and a developed, emancipated soul can never again clothe itself with flesh and blood.

The babe holds within its tiny self all wisdom, all love, all truth. That chubby little hand holds within its grasp the great universal whole for all things that are or ever shall be.

For it, countless worlds roll in space.

To it, the sun, moon and stars pay their homage.

For it, the oceans rock their cradles.

For it, the lofty mountains crest their heads.

To it, all nature bends the knee.

Creation all runs in spiral circles. When it has reached the top of one spiral, it has become too large to go back the same way it traveled. It must enter upon a new and larger spiral circle.

The wisest chemist that ever lived can never work outside of natural law. He is a servant of higher natural laws, and not their master. Do his best and he cannot make a tree or plant grow with its roots in the air and its branches buried beneath the soil.

Man's faith in immortality, which is not merely blind faith, but certainty, is as the strong wings of the flying bird that buoy him up. It fills his soul with glad songs and his eyes are bright with hope and joy. *He is now an angel in the embryonic stage.* Many things must transpire before he becomes a fully developed angel. The babe must first grow into a boy, then a Man. *So the angel must be developed, carefully and gradually from Man.*

Attraction, which is another name for love, is the secret moving spring of all creation. Without attraction or love, all things will fall into chaos.

There really is no such thing as "higher" or "lower". Such terms are merely relative. The earth is round or globular and is rolling with great rapidity in space. Consequently, there can be no such thing as higher or lower.

Life is complex, beginning with the simplest forms and ending with the greatest and grandest. Man came from the pure fountain of life, or the fountain of soul germs which do not originate either within matter or spirit. *He returns to that from which he was taken as a developed entity, or soul.*

If Man is intelligent, he came from an intelligent source or he could not be intelligent. He is simply a spark of intelligence, developed or progressed. The stream cannot rise above the fountain.

Matter runs in infinite circles from infinite atoms to infinite worlds.

Spirit runs in infinite circles from the heart of the atom to the heart of infinity. And soul runs in circles from the living germ of the moss to that of Man, angel, archangel and god angel

A certain amount of intelligence dwells within all things that have life. The least life has the least little spark, while the greatest amount that one is cognizant of dwells within mankind. And thus it is, from the atom to the angel and the god angel.

There are other worlds that hold beings who are as far beyond Man in intelligence as he is beyond the least mite of intelligence that exists on earth. All worlds in space move in strict time, perfect rhythm and heavenly harmony. Each moves within its own measure. The music of the spheres is not a figure of speech…

All things grow by being fed, commencing with the first germinal point of a world. A person's body grows by constant feeding. A person's soul and spirit grows by being fed. This great law holds good throughout all nature's domains. Starve a Man's body and it perishes. Starve a Man's mind and he becomes a fool. Take any natural light away from him and he suffers in consequence. A fool cannot rule a wise Man and if the thing is tried it becomes a failure.

When a Man looks abroad over nature's domain and finds that without a single exception, *all things grow and come into existence from a little germ or seed, and that its development depends entirely on its being constantly fed, (or its power of attraction and holding atoms together),* it stands to reason to think the globe on which he stands came into existence in the same manner. The countless worlds which he can see when he looks at the sun, moon and stars came to be by the same great universal law.

If Man could find a solitary exception to this law, there might be a loophole of escape, but there is not one instance throughout nature's domain. When he examines a rock, he finds it a conglomeration of atoms. When he examines the sand or the soil, he finds sand to be pulverized rock and the soil a compound of pulverized rock, decayed vegetation and animal refuse. When he examines the water, he finds it a gathering together of drops or atoms. All vegetation, from the least to the greatest, springs forth from a germ and grows by being fed. All insect and animal life grows in the same way. **Man, *the highest result of earth,*** grows in precisely the same way.

*As previously stated, **all things grow. All things come forth from a germ.*** This is plain, pure reason. This is the first great natural law that has no exceptions. ***The second great law is male and female, positive and negative.*** Nothing in nature springs forth from one parent alone. ***There never was a Man born on earth who did not have a father and a mother.*** There never existed an animal that did not have a father and a mother. Not an insect, not a worm, not a fish in the sea.

Some of the very lowest reptile and insect life bear the male and female in one form, but the principle is precisely the same. The same principle holds good in all vegetable life. And the atoms that compose rocks and the soil hold the male and female principle within each one. ***There is not one exception to this great law. Whenever Man finds a law that has no exception, he may commence at one end of the chain and follow it as far as his reason can go and he will make no mistake.*** When a Man uses his reason, fables fall to the ground.

If all the rolling worlds came into being through the great unchangeable law of growth and development, and one thing is gradually evolved from another, can Man find anything on earth or in the air that has not been evolved from something that existed before it? He cannot.

The law is unchangeable. ***And each evolution is higher than that which preceded it.*** Then, is not reason's chain complete, when it commences with an atom holding within itself the male and female principle, positive and negative force, or rather magnetism and matter?

Whatever the terms may be, the principle is the same. *He follows the atoms up without a break until worlds are formed.* Water is evolved from the primary rock, air from the water, ether from the air; then, commencing with decaying rock, vegetation is evolved, animal from the vegetable, Man from animal, angel from Man. The chain of reason is complete without a break.

How pure and simple all this and yet, how great, how grand, how vast. *There is no beginning, there is no end—the chain is a circle!* Man's reason can commence with one link of the chain and follow the circle, but he can find no beginning and no end.

Man was evolved from beast, and beast from vegetable and vegetable from rock, which is earth or the dust of the ground, or the dust of the rock or the decaying, or pulverized rock. It is by the separation of the male and female principle which resides within one germinal form at first, into two forms, that the Man and Woman do exist in their present state. And so of all animals as well.

God and heaven do really have an existence but not in the general acceptation of the term. Man's reason is wisdom and wisdom is reason. The lack of it, or not using it, is error and error is fable or falsehood. Therefore, the fool exercises faith or the belief in fables without reason, for the lack of reason makes the Man a fool. A fool is faith without reason and reason is wisdom or God...

INVOLUTION AND EVOLUTION

All things tend upward, together with Man.

A soul germ or germ of anything, after being once developed, can never, under any circumstances, return again to the germinal state. Every child born on the face of the earth, or any earth, was, before being inhaled by the father, a spiritual or soul germ floating in ethereal space. Germs may not be visible to all persons, but they are visible to many. As each germ can never be anything but itself, and each child born on earth can never be anything than itself, a developed spiritual or soul germ, consequently a fully matured soul germ, could not enter the body of an infant, for that infant is a germ itself in process of development.

The human body changes entirely once in 7 years. If every atom of matter within a Man's body is renewed every 7 years, that is *after 7 years,* there is not one atom of the old body remaining. Then it is not possible that the germs of his future children still remain, for every atom of his body has been renewed.

As each 7 years roll around, not an atom of the old remains. Before puberty, he had not even the power of generation—such power did not reside within his body. Man gets the new atoms from which to make up his new body every seven years from the foods he eats, the water he drinks and the air he breathes. Water alone will not sustain him. Food alone will not sustain him. Added to these, he must have air and plenty of it. He can live without food for many days. He can live without water for a considerable time, but he cannot live ten minutes in a conscious, breathing state without air. He does not obtain the souls of his future children from the foods he eats. His food is dead matter, devoid of soul or spirit. He does not obtain them from the water he drinks. The germs of the human soul do not reside within water as water, but they do reside within the air. All the food he eats and all the water he drinks cannot even make blood until, through the lungs, air comes in contact with it. Man depends entirely on the air to even form the blood in his veins and, in seven years not an item of the old body remains, not even a drop of the old blood.

Living germs are constantly being breathed in by the male parent. *They are developed or clothed in his blood* until they have sufficient strength to enter a prepared ovum. As material forms progress, they attract and breathe in correspondingly higher germs. That is, a donkey cannot attract and hold the germs that are intended to develop into a perfect Man but a very fine ape can breathe in and hold the germs that are a shade higher and finer than the creature that inhales them. As fast as these forms progress, they attract and hold higher and still higher germs.

The soul germs of children enter the lungs of the male parent with the air that is breathed. From the lungs, they enter the blood, passing through the heart with every pulsation. The germs then commence to clothe themselves with material substance in the father's blood. *All hereditary tendencies come from the clothing the spiritual germ takes on and are not in the pure spiritual germ itself. Heredity is all in matter and not in the pure spirit.* These germs are as indestructible as the ether in which they reside. Those that do not find an opportunity to develop simply escape all environments, just as the air and ether escape that which they reside, from the lungs and from all parts and pores of the body. All germs are simply clothed with matter in the blood of the father. Some do not find lodgement within an egg or ovum. Therefore, that matter dies and drops away from the germ, *for the germs themselves are indestructible* and float away once more within the ethereal air.

The female inhales germs as well as the male, but she makes no use of them. They are to her simply as the air she breathes. Nature is positive and negative, male and female. *The positive force (male) holds and makes use of them. The negative force (female) repels or exhales them.*

All creatures attract, hold and make use of the germs belonging to their own species or kind. An animal cannot hold and make use of the germs of human beings. *Each attracts and holds its own kind.* A germ which forms a grain of wheat cannot form corn, or tomato. That is why things do not get mixed up more than they do.

Man's body is formed of material substance. Whole life resides within the atmosphere and his nostrils breathe it in.

Heredity is simply that which is inherited from the material with which the father or mother has clothed the germ. This is also the reason why children resemble their parents. But the soul, the inner principle is not tainted in the least for sooner or later, either in the material, spiritual or celestial life, it becomes perfect as at first. It has progressed up through the material, the spiritual and the celestial, gradually throwing off all impurities on its course until it is a God-angel or archangel or the wisest and best angel that Man can possibly conceive of.

If every Man, animal, reptile, insect, fish and all vegetable life were swept away from the earth today, all things would exist again in a comparatively short period of time in every part of the globe. The oceans, seas, rivers, ponds and lakes would be filled with fish. Insect, reptile and animal life and lastly Man would appear. This would not take place in one little spot at a time but would be simultaneous in every part of the earth. In tropical climes, evolution goes more rapidly.

The moment rock on every part of the globe crumbled slightly, enough to hold a little moisture, moss would immediately form **simultaneously** all over the globe. At the same time, the atmosphere would supply all necessary germs for the very lowest form of life within the waters. As rapidly as nature could evolve, higher and still higher forms of life would appear, nearly at the same time, provided climatic conditions were favorable. Not one Man alone, but millions of Men would appear and the world would come up into civilization then just as it has done, *the angelic world aiding it as rapidly as it was capable of being aided.*

There are millions upon millions of earth's in just a condition at the present time but there are millions upon millions of other planets that are progressed far beyond these earth's. There are countless millions of spirits and angels from these planets who can be, and are, interested in these crude earth's, working with and for them. *That is how intelligence and spirituality appear.*

The vault of heaven has countless stars which are suns to other systems of worlds that cannot be seen with the naked eye, and **all of these worlds are co-related.**

As soon as souls leave the earth, as rapidly as they gain in wisdom, they must work for and impart this wisdom to those still in the body. This is the way progress can be made. If angels simply thought of their own progress and happiness and never looked back to aid the ones left behind, they would not be worthy of wisdom or happiness and consequently, would neither be wise nor happy. They strive for knowledge and happiness then turn, or descend, and impart it to those below them. The wisest ones who have left the earth cannot be very far in advance of the wisest ones of earth, their proteges.

Spirits and angels must work, and work continually, for there are millions of spirits that are low, ignorant, debased and degraded. These must be taught as well as the people of the earth's. They must give of their knowledge and happiness almost as fast as it can be received.

It is sometimes thought that if Man has a soul that continues to exist after the body is dissolved, he attained it through the process of evolution. **Nothing can be evolved that did not previously exist.** It is sometimes thought that mind evolves from matter—that matter is gradually molded up into mind, then into spirit and then into immortal soul. This theory of evolution is but half true. **A speck of protoplasm or matter cannot take unto itself any form whatever without the soul germs. The soul germs are distinct entities.** They never evolve one type into another type or one type will never evolve from a different type.

Eternity is filled with these soul germs, as it is also filled with matter and spirit. Eternity consists of three primary principles: matter, spirit and soul. At first they are all minute points or atoms: a minute point of pure flame, or spirit, a minute point of matter, or clothing, and a minute point of soul or germ. *The soul germ is that which fashions and makes use of, or covers itself, with spirit and matter. All soul germs, or germs of life, no matter how low in the scale they might be, are distinct entities and cannot develop into anything but their own distinct individuality.* One form of life makes the conditions for a higher form to appear, making it possible for the next grade of soul germs to take up the matter which the former threw down after fully developing into all that nature designed them to be.

If evolution were true, one Man or race of men might gradually evolve into another. *Races do not evolve one from another or one into another.* A white race can never be evolved from a black one, never under any circumstances. That they mix slightly, up to a certain point is true, but beyond that point, or limit, *they cannot go.*

The American Indian does not evolve. Nor the African Negro, the Chinese and so on. They can never evolve gradually into a white race. As a race, they will die but they never evolve. A horse and a donkey may be crossed but can go no further. There will be a hybrid or mule and that is the limit. The mule ceases to propagate or evolve.

The Chinese nation has been on the earth millions of years. That nation never evolved into anything but the Chinese. If China is conquered by other nations, the Chinese may die, but they will not evolve. They will never become a white nation. It is admitted that nations mix slightly, but this does not continue. *They die out as nations. The tendency is ever to return to that form from which they sprung.* The climate and conditions favor certain species to the exclusion of others, but *the germs are forever true to themselves* and naturally gravitate, or are attracted to, the country or climate favorable to their growth

The ape made it possible for the soul germs of Mankind to at length be inhaled and develop as men on earth, but all nations did

71

not have the same root. The soul germ of no Man ever came from an ape. The highest possible ape was able to inhale and make use of a germ a shade higher than itself. In this sense, evolution is true and half true. The whole truth is involution *and* evolution.

Races of men and different species of animals do not run into each other. All nations are graded and exist as nations, distinct nations in the germinal state. When a nation has reached the development which nature designed for it, it disappears or dies out. And so of all species of animal, insect and reptile life. So of all vegetable and floral life. When the earth has no further need of horses, they will cease to exist or die out. And so of all other animals; and, as the ages roll on, Man himself will also disappear from the earth. All these things, together with Man, will be simply moved onward and upward into a higher state or condition.

Man, while developing within the material, needs all that is developed within the material. When he reaches the spiritual or celestial, he needs all that the earth has developed which he considers beneath himself and can no more get along without it in the spirit world then he can in the material world.

Neither spirit nor soul can ever be evolved from matter. Spirit is spirit forever. Soul is soul forever. Matter is matter forever. A thing cannot be evolved from that which it does not have.

SPIRITUAL EVOLUTION

The spiritual world is sublimated and attenuated matter.

It is not Man alone who is translated to a spiritual life, but everything which surrounds Man on earth. All things tend upward, together with Man. In the spiritual world he may have his house, his garden and his flowers. He may live in a city, village, town or in the country. He may sail on water or visit forests, mountains, valleys and glens. He may visit different races of men, as well as planets and constellations of worlds. Oftentimes Man can hardly realize that he is not on the material plane of being. The only difference he finds is that all things are now spiritual, devoid of gross matter. The spiritual world is really material after all, *for spirit clothes itself with sublimated matter, and the earthly world is gross matter. The spiritual world is sublimated matter.* There is no place throughout eternity that is devoid of matter, either in its gross or sublimated form. There is no place throughout eternity that is devoid of spirit. There is no spot throughout eternity that is devoid of soul. Spirit and matter are but the handmaidens of soul, *and soul is creator: the living and governing principle with all that exists or has life.*

In the spiritual world are all races and various tribes of men. The lines are drawn with more distinction than on the earth. The various races abide together by themselves, mingling very little with those not belonging to them. Their cities and towns are usually over and above the corresponding cities and towns of earth. More especially is this true of the spheres nearest earth. For instance, over and above the Chinese Empire exist innumerable spiritual stratas, nearly all made up of the native Chinese. So too of Africa. So of Egypt. So of India. So of the islands of the sea. So of Europe. So of America, both North and South. This is also true of the various cities and towns, especially of the large cities of the world.

This must necessarily be so. But this does not mean that spirits and angels may not and do not go whenever and wherever they please. Still, this general law holds good and the natural law of attraction and adaptability holds nations and tribes together. The Chinese are Chinese still. The Hindus are still Hindus. The African is African still, and so on. This law holds good throughout eternity. An individual holds his individuality throughout eternity. So do nations and races of men.

The earth herself is but a small nucleus within her spheres, and together her spheres are many, very many thousand times larger than her gross material bulk. She travels this enormous orbital pathway, leaving behind each year tokens that she has been there. Her very outermost sublimated sphere is partly left behind each year, all that she cannot hold any longer by her attractive force. These various forms of youth and beauty are gradually filling immensity.

The zodiac is bordered in all directions, millions upon millions of miles each way, by the spiritual emanations thrown off from the earth. There are scenes upon scenes of heaven. These are of such transcendent and surpassing loveliness that they cannot be described.

Man's idea of heaven is not meaningless. It is at first crude and not well understood, but time remedies that. There are many other facets of this subject that Man does not comprehend, such as that the earth's pathway is never precisely the same, or that the sun is traveling also and carrying her children, the planets, with her. The spheres are those which the earth carries with her: the zones are that which she leaves behind in her zodiacal pathway around the sun. This describes the earth, not to mention the other planets, and only pertains to one relatively small planet.

Spirits can ascend and descend. Yet, it is true that all angels make their homes in the celestial sphere which corresponds with their wisdom and love.

The spiritual atmosphere is something more than ether. It is ethereal, but more dense or different from the fundamental ether. This is pertaining to the spiritual spheres around the earth which go with it in its revolutions, held to it by the law of attraction. If there were nothing but ether to attract, there would be no spiritual spheres at all, for the ether extends throughout all space and holds no more attraction for one planet than for another. Consequently, there would be nothing to be attracted. The spiritual spheres must consist of something tangible, or the earth could not hold them around it. There must be, as there is, tangible matter that can be attracted—inhaled by the great law of attraction. As previously stated, *all space whatever is filled by matter, spirit, and germinal points and all space whatever is filled with ether.* There is no such thing as 'void' or 'nothing'. Spiritual spheres are composed of sublimated or attenuated matter, which is nevertheless solid enough to attract and be attracted, else spirit must simply roam through ether, intangible and consequently without form. Natural law is forever striving to bring forth forms of beauty, intelligence and youth. The higher the spheres, the more pronounced and unmistakable is this law. **When matter becomes too ethereal to be attracted by the earth, it is thrown off into the great zone of the earth's orbit.**

By the law of involution, all things are evolved. The involuting of spiritual germs is that which is to be evolved. Man is "involved" as the germ of a Man and then "evolved" as a Man: the germ develops and is perfected within matter and from there evolved into the celestial spheres.

A spiritual being cannot travel to far distant spheres. A spiritual body cannot travel faster than light, but within this body is another body called the "thought body" which can do these things. Not the soul, for within this thought body dwells the soul. A person on earth who has not yet laid aside the material body has a material body, a spiritual body, a thought body and a soul. The soul is the immortal living principle that has neither beginning nor end and it clothes itself with these various bodies or substances: the material body, the spiritual body and the thought body. It expresses itself through these various forms.

The material body cannot leave the material earth, and yet the thought body can transfer itself instantaneously to any part of the globe as well as to the far away regions in space. The spiritual body, after leaving the material body, cannot leave the spiritual spheres, but the thought body can go, in a comparatively short time, to any sphere or zone that it is possible to cognize. But, *when the spirit is freed from the earthly body, its powers are increased a hundredfold and its perceptions and sight become clear and lucid.*

The soul has the power of freeing itself of the spiritual body for quite lengthy periods of time. The spiritual body goes to sleep, or becomes unconscious, while the soul and thought body fly away to other zones.

Thought can travel as fast as electricity—and even faster. The brain is really a storage battery. It not only sends forth its currents of thought but it is a receiver at the same time.

Examine the sun on a very warm and sunny day. It is rapidly drawing the sweet life and essence out of the vegetation. This ascends and fills the air. This substance, or vapor, rises far above the watery clouds before condensing. It does not condense in the same way that water does, but seems to spread itself out in thin sheets, or layers, one above the other. The lower, or coarser portion which the sun has drawn up keeps gradually falling away from the finer or higher, and falls, at last, back into the earth's atmosphere.

Ascending into the higher portion, if one could mingle with it, a kind of thin, phantom representation of all things which the sun kisses is there. This ethereal, or phantom mist, rises higher and higher until it rests upon the earth's atmosphere and now is within the spirit world. The dying rose of earth had at first sent a thin spiritual film upward, and, as the rose faded, the *spiritual* rose grew bright and beautiful, **nourished and fed by its own ambrosial nectar.** Thus it is of all the trees, flowers, grasses and shrubs in the spiritual realm. Every flower and shrub and tree is absorbed, **to retain its original identity.**

All things separate each to its own order or kingdom, just as things on earth, for all the spiritual spheres of earth are fed from the earth. **The earth is the great reservoir, or feeder of the realms which rise above and surround it.** Vegetation, grass, trees and flowers yield up their lives more slowly than the animal and insect kingdom do, for the animal kingdom is higher than the vegetable or floral. The animal yields up his life, or spirit, at once and rises rapidly upward.

It does not pause until it strikes the spirit land. The animal has a certain amount of intelligence and find its place according to its attractions. A wild animal immediately seeks a dense, spiritual forest. A domestic animal often pauses near a spiritual home, or revels in the green meadows, or wanders beside the running streams and rivers, or gazes with its large dewy eyes at the lakes. The birds wing their way, as on earth, singing their sweet songs. They love to linger near the habitations of men, the same as on earth. The insects also gravitate to their natural places.

As the spheres rise one above the other, and as the earth is the nucleus or center, there is room enough for all and room to spare, for this first sphere above the earth is correspondingly larger than the earth. And so they go on enlarging. And when, at last, the outermost sphere is reached, the distance from the nucleus, or earth, is quite astounding and its circumference more astounding still. Even when that is at last reached, there remains the earth's orbit or it's inconceivable pathway around the sun, which is also a vast zone of spiritual life and beauty.

Within the spheres, there is no propagation proper. *All spiritual forms come from the earth, or all spiritual germs must develop within matter and, as they develop and throw off their coarse covering, they rise into the spiritual realm.*

GOD

The hands which formed the visible universe.

Before worlds could be attracted and held together in the form of globes, magnetism and matter existed. Magnetism and matter existed—or do exist—in a state where they are not in the form of a globe.

A globe is merely the effect of a previous cause. Matter and magnetism existed in a nude state before they took on the form of globes.

One cannot see matter before it is held together by magnetism in the form of a globe, or innumerable globes. Magnetism and matter both exist in an invisible state, or at least invisible to Man.

Now we have a king and a queen: invisible magnetism and invisible matter. We will crown them by wedding them: *The Creator is a trinity.*

We have been analyzing first principles or the hands which formed the visible universe. These are the *invisible* hands of Creator.

We have analyzed the two hands of The Creator but *magnetism nor matter has not intelligent life within it.*

Neither magnetism nor matter is intelligent, even in their first or invisible state. Intelligence is not magnetism and is not matter. Pure magnetism and pure matter united can bring forth no greater results than globular form, unaided by a third principle.

Now, we wed the king and queen. Magnetism is the queen, matter is the king. *Intelligence* is the high priest or fountainhead—the godhead.

Intelligence makes Man think. *Undeveloped intelligence resides within all life.* One can very easily trace its development. The germ, which at length develops into a babe, was breathed in by the father from the atmosphere. If *intelligence exists in the form of invisible undeveloped germs,* along with invisible magnetism and invisible matter, the king and queen are then crowned with intelligence.

All three are invisible until they are manifested in the visible.

There is not only creator God but a triune creator God, creator of the heavens and the earth—creator of the sun, moon and stars. Here is the Trinity; not exactly as Father, Son and Holy Ghost, but *intelligence, magnetism and matter.* Bride, bridegroom and high priest. *An invisible, eternal God..!*

Nature toils for countless ages to develop intelligence. Take a leaf or flower for example. The unplucked leaf yields up its spirit or immortal part while it is on the tree. It is developed or spiritual form and, until it yields its spirit up, the leaf remains intact, or in a rapidly developing condition.

As the leaf becomes perfectly developed, it commences to yield up its spirit, or die as it is called. When all the life and beauty has departed from it, it casts down to earth about two-thirds of its proper weight. It is robbed of all life and spirit. The life, or spirit of the leaf, does not fall to earth at all. On the contrary, it takes its proper place within the atmosphere. To an observer, it appears as though the withered leaf on the ground again returns to dust. It merely appears thus for a while.

Disintegration goes on very slowly with it but *when every atom which composes it has been robbed of all the spirit, then the atoms also rise into the atmosphere; but they are worthless; they have no spirit within them.* All worthless atoms at length rise and are pushed outside the atmosphere. There they lie in helpless masses for a season.

Even the worthless or worn out atoms cannot return to their first or primary condition any more than a Man can return to his babyhood. This is true of matter and true of spirit.

Glass is made from sand. One may grind glass to the finest powder, and it will never be sand again. The material of which all vegetation is composed, when once it has entered into the composition of vegetable growth, will never return to its first, or primary condition. *All the atoms that have been robbed of their spirit will eventually rise outside the atmosphere.*

Prairie fires may blaze year after year, but one cannot find the ashes. A farmer understands this well. After a few years, his cultivated land becomes worthless and will not yield even grass unless new spirit is put into it. The land yields up its spirit to vegetation, vegetation yields up its spirit to animal life or to the atmosphere, and animal life yields up its spirit to intelligent life, or to the atmosphere. *Intelligence never again returns to undeveloped intelligence.* Always forward, never backwards. It enters the (to Man) invisible world as developed intelligence.

All forms are not resolved into their first or elementary state, they never can be. A developed form can never return to its first condition, no more than a Man can ever again become a babe. All forms are developed from an invisible germ, but a developed germ can never again become an undeveloped germ.

As the germ develops, it robs the matter with which it clothes itself of its spirit. The matter thus impoverished never returns to its first estate, neither does the spirit. *One, in developing, has robbed the other.*

Matter and magnetism are equally blended within all forms. When the undeveloped germ of intelligence once takes root within magnetism and matter, *it feeds upon them and grows until it is fully developed.*

When it no longer needs matter, it casts it off. This matter, thus robbed of its magnetism, becomes inert and worthless and, at length is pushed outside the atmosphere. The developed intelligence, clothed in its living garb of magnetism, also rises to the unseen or spiritual realm.

All things that are or ever shall be are God. God works in, and with and through all things. We each individually have as much of God as we are capable of holding. We are parts and parcels of God, as are all other things that exist, as well as suns, moons, and stars and all life whatever contained thereon. *That* is to understand God and walk with him (or her, or the oneness of the male and female) in all the workings of the universe. *Nothing within the universe moves without an unseen force to move it.*

One cannot see the power or the willpower which causes one to lift his arm or the motive power which moves the brain. It is invisible and does not cease with the death of the body. While one lives, the body is warm. One cannot see heat or cold yet they are the most prevalent forces in the universe. Heat and cold are real although invisible forces.

The magnetic body within a Man, which animates the electric body and forever hides within it, *is the secret cause of the pulsing heart.*

It is the spirit within a Man which pulses, and *magnetism, or spiritual flame, is the motive power.* Therefore, your heart still beats and will keep on beating while the eternal ages roll...

What causes a bird to fly? The bird's mind, or will power, causes it to fly. In earth life, it has a heavy material body. Therefore, it must be supplied with a material battery and electric wires running to every part of the frame. The material battery is it's brain, and it's nerves are the wires. The battery (brain) is worked by it's mind or will power which sends currents of electricity all along the different sets of wires (nerves) which it desires to move, and when it is flying, the motive power is electricity. The motive power which causes it to fly is electricity, *and so of all motion whatever.*

A person rows a boat in the same way. The boat is a separate thing from the rower, while the bird's body is its own. The boat has no nerves like the wing of a bird. And an oar, such as men use for propelling small boats, has no nerves yet it is moved by an arm, and an oar in turn moves the boat. Yet, there is no mind or nerve, within the oar but the boat, the oar, and the Man's arms are all connected in such a way that the boat is propelled by electricity—the electricity running on the nerves, or wires, of the arm of the Man. His mind, or willpower governs it and every independent motion which the boat makes.

It is the resisting power of the water which propels the boat. Without that, the boat would not move despite the efforts which the Man puts forth.

In the spiritual realm the resisting force is not the water, but the atmosphere, the spiritual atmosphere which is ether. Ether, or the ethereal atmosphere, resists or retards electricity, or electric rays.

The spiritual being shoots the electric rays from his mind, or willpower. The ethereal atmosphere acts just as water does on earth, it resists the rays. *Magnetism and electricity are the motive powers which move all the worlds in space as well as are the cause of all light and heat. When heat has departed from a Man, he is so-called dead.*

All things are not as they appear to mortal sight. Man should think of himself as residing on a solid hub, or nucleus, which is in rapid motion. This is surrounded by a dense atmosphere with corresponding movement. Over and around these are the ethereal or spiritual and angelic spheres which move correspondingly with the rest, like a wheel with many rims, each larger than the last, with spaces between corresponding with the earth's atmosphere. The atmosphere rests upon the earth, the first spiritual sphere rests upon the atmosphere. More ethereal spheres rest upon that, and so on. All move with the hub as it revolves.

This immense wheel, like innumerable other wheels of its kind, rolls within the eternal ocean of matter and spirit which exist forever and ever without end. From this eternal ocean, countless worlds are formed by the great eternal law of attraction, or the uniting of spirit and matter. Man is yet finite, and the finite may not grasp the infinite but must reach it by gradual and easy growth.

The time is near when the people on this earth ball will become aware of a real tangible heaven, one that they can be as sure of as they are of their present existence on the earth, or, as they are of the clouds that float in the atmosphere about them. Not a visionary happening beyond the stars, but a real heaven surrounding and embracing them, one that the earth herself has yielded up and is constantly yielding up.

A heaven which the earth is forming, and has been forming ever since she has been capable of evolving anything. We can follow the chain without a break or mistake until we arrive at a point where the finite mind can go no farther.

The great law of evolution itself goes on throughout eternity. If Man evolves his spirit, then all nature evolves its spirit. If Man rises to a spiritual altitude, then the spirit of all nature rises to its altitude, the same as the clouds rise to their altitude. If heat expands and carries water to a certain level and leaves it in the form of clouds, the same vehicle—heat—expands and carries the essence of all natural or growing things that passed through that which is called death, to their proper altitude. There it leaves them while *heat itself (which is but the electric rays from the sun) rushes onto its own altitude and loses itself in the vast magnetic globe which lies directly opposed to the sun* and is invisible to Man.

A flower or a leaf dies. All its life and beauty depart from it. Nothing but a dry husk remains. The essences are resolved into the atmosphere. They are *evolved* into the atmosphere. One may think that the constituents of the flower or leaf pass again into other flowers. Such is not the eternal law of evolution.

There is a power, call it God or any other name, that fills all immensity. All that is, all that ever was or all that ever shall be is God.

God sits enthroned within his own body—for *God and the soul of Man are one and the same. The soul of Man first exists as an invisible germ within a little invisible magnetic and electric globe—male and female in one.* Therefore, *God is both male and female, equally balanced and co-existent...*

Positive and negative or male and female are a great, eternal, immutable law. There is not one exception throughout Nature's vast domain. There is nothing that is not male and female or positive and negative. It is the uniting, or marriage, of the male and female principles in nature that **creates all things.**

Nothing is created or comes into being except the uniting of the male and female principles, or positive and negative forces. **There is not one solitary exception to this great law. The uniting of male and female, or positive and negative forces, is the creator of all that is, or was, or ever shall be and the Creator is male and female equally balanced and coexistent.**

Therefore, God is male **and** female and all form or creation results from the union. If all creation is God and God is the eternal whole, then the soul of Man must find an abiding place within God, or within creation somewhere.

As all things are evolved, one from another, and there is no exception to the law, then Man's future abiding place must be evolved **from his present condition.** His surroundings must be evolved from his present surroundings, his spirit must be evolved from his body, and his spiritual home must be evolved from his earthly one.

The law of evolution never turns backward, but always takes its step in advance. It never takes a stride, but a modest step. Man's first spiritual condition cannot be but a simple modest step in advance of this.

The dense atmosphere rests upon the earth. The first spiritual sphere rests upon that atmosphere, is evolved entirely from the earth and is composed of the earths emanations as they are carried up through the atmosphere by heat, the electrical rays of the sun. These spiritual emanations are left at their proper altitude just as water is carried up by heat in the form of vapor and left at *its* proper altitude.

All water that is carried up does not fall back to earth. Much of the water that arises becomes so attenuated and etherealized, that it rises above the dense atmosphere and takes its appointed place within the spiritual sphere.

When the spirit of Man rises up to its natural abode in the heavens, he finds rivers, seas, lakes and oceans. Not heavy and dense but rare, ethereal, attenuated and spiritualized precisely as he is spiritualized. It is as real to him as the more compact, dense, heavy waters of earth are to his compact, dense, heavy and material body.

Of all else that the earth produces, *the spiritual part of all things ascends,* and all that which is called death is ascension, or *evolution*—merely taking a step higher, that is all.

In the natural abode of the heavens, the things produced through the mind of Man are first his dwellings then all things which he invents or manufactures for his comfort and convenience. Then, paintings and musical instruments. There is scarcely any limit to his inventions. Things do not cease when he takes a step higher. He erects, invents, becomes wise, paints finer pictures, evolves instruments of greater perfection, and so on *ad infinitum.*

When we find a law that has no exception whatever we are safe in concluding that the law never did have an exception and never will. It is eternal and we can follow it out to its ultimate and make no mistake.

All things whatever start from a germinal point. There is no exception to this law, not even in Man. He also starts in the same way. He is the highest product of the earth. This law is forever and eternal.

All form whatever is held together by magnetism, or magnetic attraction, and that magnetism exists throughout all space forever and is eternal. It exists in fine invisible points of pure magnetic flame. Each point attracts and holds firmly a covering of matter. **Nothing** *can take on a form without first attracting and holding a spiritual germ.*

All forms whatever are composed of magnetism which is invisible, and matter which is visible, and the spiritual germ, which can be seen, and which holds within itself the exact form, in miniature, of the form which it develops. As it develops, it clothes itself with magnetism in matter.

Magnetism is the spiritual dress and matter is the material garb. As soon as it becomes perfectly developed, it blossoms and the blossoms attract and hold other germs *like itself.* At last it grows old and dies. It has become a perfect form and performed its mission. Then it is ready to take its place higher up in the ascending scale.

It is the germ which has developed and, in developing, has clothed itself with magnetism and matter. The magnetic flame is the germ's inner or spiritual clothing and matter is its outer, or material, clothing. The developed germ has no further use for its material clothing. In fact, it is a clog which deters it from rising higher in the scale. Therefore, it leaves it, or shakes it off. But the developed germ still holds fast to its magnetic clothing. *It cannot part with this.* Magnetism is its vehicle as well as its spiritual clothing. The developed germ rises up to its proper attitude in its perfected form, clothed with its magnetic garment. All forms of whatever kind that exist follow the same great law, and thus the spiritual universes are formed. They are composed of all the developed forms that exist on the earth or on other earths.

There is a great mistake made in thinking that all forms are, at death, resolved back into their elementary condition. All forms are developed germs, which are eternal. A developed germ is never resolved back into an undeveloped germ. That is impossible. ***The sole reason of its development is to form universes of perfect imperishable*** _beauty—that the highest product of all, Man's intelligent soul may have a home in every way fitted to his needs._

The germs of all forms whatever exist within space, or have and ever will. They develop up through magnetism and matter into their full forms. They then cast off matter and ascend to the first spiritual sphere, which is not probably more than 5 to 10 miles distant, and rest upon the atmosphere of the earth.

Consequently, the first sphere must be five or ten times larger than the earth. All developed forms ascend to this sphere and form a world of imperishable and perfect beauty wherein Man's soul, clothed in his spiritual dress of gauzy magnetism, roams at his own sweet will and pleasure. He finds there all natural objects which he has been accustomed to see on earth: a spiritual earth, insects, animals, plants, trees and vegetation of all kinds developing according to their kind. Man develops according to his kind.

Again, there can be no break in this law. **If Man is immortal, so are all things else.** If Man develops and ripens for immortality through the materiality, so do all things else that have life, whatever their kind. All things die, or cast off their material covering. It is against all reason to suppose that man is alone in his immortality. If all germs exist previous to inception, it is impossible for them not to exist after development.

When we leave this material covering, we shall find a world of immortal beauty made up of the developed forms of all life which we have here. It is beautiful and natural that Man should ascend together with all that he has lived with and associated with here. Nature as well as his art does not leave him, they ascend with him...

Printed in the United States
By Bookmasters